THE DISEASE BOOK

THE
DISEASE
BOOK

A Kids' Guide

Margaret O. Hyde

AND

Elizabeth H. Forsyth, M.D.

Illustrations by Bari Weissman

WALKER AND COMPANY • *New York*

97 2993

This book is not intended to be a substitute for medical advice,
which should be given by a doctor, but it can help you develop a
better partnership with your doctor and answer many questions
about diseases, new and old.

First published in the United States of America in 1997 by
Walker Publishing Company, Inc.

Published simultaneously in Canada by Thomas Allen & Son
Canada, Limited, Markham, Ontario

Library of Congress Cataloging-in-Publication Data
Hyde, Margaret O. (Margaret Oldroyd)
The disease book: a kids' guide/Margaret O. Hyde and Elizabeth
H. Forsyth.
p. cm.
Includes bibliographical references and index.
Summary: Discusses the causes, symptoms, effects, and treat-
ment of a variety of diseases and disorders arranged under such
categories as "Disorders of the Lungs," "Mental Illness," and
"Disorders of the Digestive System."
ISBN 0-8027-8497-6 (hc).   —ISBN 0-8027-8498-4
1. Medicine—Juvenile literature.   2. Diseases—Juvenile
literature.   3. Children—Diseases—Juvenile literature.
[1. Diseases.   2. Medical care.]   I. Forsyth, Elizabeth Held.
II. Title.
R130.5.H94   1997
616—dc21   97-155
CIP
AC

Book design by Dede Cummings

Diagrams on pages 5, 14, 31, 48, 86, and 87 by Jon Forsyth

Printed in the United States of America
2   4   6   8   10   9   7   5   3   1

To
Ben R. Forsyth, M.D.
Pierre B. Fayad, M.D.
John F. Setaro, M.D.

Contents

Introduction

About 25,000 diseases exist, with cures for about 5,000 of them. They range from those as common as acne to those as uncommon as xerosis (abnormal dryness of the skin). The common cold is a nuisance; Ebola fever is exotic, fascinating, and lethal. Diseases are steeped in myth, the subject of extensive and expensive research, and seemingly ever present.

Medicine has come a long way since the days when people thought of diseases as the acts of angry gods or the curses of witches. Some diseases that seem unimportant today played a large role in history. For example, measles caused widespread illness and death in the ancient empires of Rome and China, but now there are fewer than 1,000 cases a year in the United States. Throughout history, epidemics of diseases such as the Black Death (bubonic plague), cholera, and smallpox cut down large populations. Today, many of these killer diseases are rare, and smallpox has been completely eradicated worldwide. But in spite of spectacular progress in the world of medicine, cancer, blood and heart diseases, stroke, and certain infectious diseases are still sending large numbers of people to their graves.

In any group of people, many diseases are represented. Lifestyle plays a part in the development of some diseases, but heredity and other factors are usually involved, too.

Mel is hoping that new AIDS drugs will appear before his disease reaches the last stages. He is now taking fourteen pills each day, and his condition is getting worse. There are spots on his skin from a form of cancer called Kaposi's sarcoma; he is blind, his body is wasting away, and his weakened immune system is no longer able to fight off infections. But new treatments have been adding years to the lives of people with AIDS, and Mel has lived longer than he had thought he would. HIV, the virus that causes AIDS, is still a lethal infection, but it is no longer an immediate death sentence. More than 4,000 different conditions, such as cystic fibrosis and sickle cell anemia, are caused by inborn damage to genes. Many other ailments, such as heart disease, cancer, and arthritis, have some genetic basis.

New methods of prevention and treatment have changed the course of many diseases, but not all can be cured. Some linger for long periods or even for a lifetime. These are called chronic diseases, and they remain the greatest cause of death.

Infectious diseases are diseases caused by viruses, bacteria, parasites, and other living organisms. While some are rare, others are on the rise. The vaccines and antibiotics that were used to control them gave hope a few years ago of a world in which infectious diseases were brought under control. But that hope is fading as doctors report an international resurgence in a variety of infectious diseases.

A sharp increase in antibiotic-resistant strains of germs that cause pneumonia, meningitis, tuberculosis, cholera, typhus, malaria, and other diseases is also being reported regularly. Suppose you are infected with a kind of microbe called staphylococcus after an operation in a large hospital. Today, the variety that infects you may be the "staph" that is immune to every kind of antibiotic but one. What will happen when it becomes resistant to that antibiotic?

The most serious threat of infection comes from the

many germs that live normally in the body and cause disease when your resistance is lowered. Even biting your own finger may result in disease. One bacterium in your body can multiply into 16,777,220 bacteria within a day, and some of the new ones can carry a mutant gene that is resistant to common antibiotics. When some of these new strains are spread to other people, a huge public health problem may arise.

Even though everyone in the world has or has had some infectious diseases, many of these disorders are still not well understood. While some of the old diseases have been conquered, new threats such as AIDS, Lyme disease, Lassa fever, Ebola fever, and drug-resistant tuberculosis have become a challenge. Deaths from infectious diseases rose from the fifth leading cause of death in 1980 to the third in 1992. Even when AIDS and HIV-related diseases were not counted, deaths from infectious diseases rose 22 percent in that period.

Infectious disease specialists are currently hard at work trying to control a killer strain of cholera in Southeast Asia, a form of diphtheria that is raging in Russia, and the eternal problems of diseases spread by travelers from one part of the globe to another. Even changes in climate can affect the amount of disease. The number of cases of malaria could increase between 7 and 28 percent if conditions for the mosquitoes that carry it are changed by global warming. Controlling the spread of diseases is a challenge on many fronts.

This book is intended to help you learn the basics about some of the many diseases that are important to young people and their families and to lead you to sources of further information. In many cases, free booklets with information about diseases mentioned here are available from various organizations listed at the end of the book. Some can be reached by a toll-free phone call and have their own web site on the Internet.

Disorders of the Heart and Blood Vessels

The heart is an amazing organ, a muscular pump that beats automatically and steadily 60 to 100 times a minute, hour after hour, day after day, year after year, delivering 2,100 gallons of blood every day to the tissues in your body. It is made up of a system of chambers and valves that forces blood into the main distributing vessels—the arteries—which supply the various organs with blood. The arteries break up into smaller and smaller branches that go inside each organ, then branch into tiny vessels called capillaries. Nutrients and oxygen from the blood pass into the tissues, and waste products pass out through their thin walls. After flowing through the capillary network, the blood is returned to the heart through the veins. If the network of arteries, veins, and capillaries in one person's body was rearranged into a continuous line, that line could circle the earth about two and a half times. In an average lifetime, the heart pumps about 1 million barrels of blood through

Heart and Major Blood Vessels

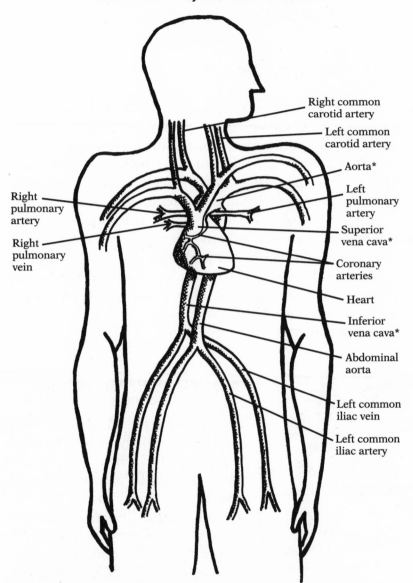

Right common carotid artery

Left common carotid artery

Aorta*

Left pulmonary artery

Superior vena cava*

Coronary arteries

Heart

Inferior vena cava*

Abdominal aorta

Left common iliac vein

Left common iliac artery

Right pulmonary artery

Right pulmonary vein

*Aorta: The body's main artery; it carries blood from the heart. *Superior vena cava:* Large vein that returns blood to the heart from the head, neck, and upper limbs. *Inferior vena cava:* Large vein that returns blood to the heart from the abdomen and lower limbs.

these vessels. The list of diseases of the heart and blood vessels is long. Here are some of the more common ones:

CONGENITAL DISORDERS

Some heart disorders are present at birth. Although their cause is usually unknown, we do know that having certain viral infections during pregnancy, such as German measles (rubella), can cause heart and other defects in the infant. Moreover, if a pregnant woman takes particular drugs, amphetamines (speed), lithium, or progesterone, for example, or drinks alcohol, her baby is also at risk. One-half of the children born to alcoholic mothers have congenital heart defects, in addition to other problems.

Congenital disorders may involve deformed valves, abnormal connections between blood vessels, and holes in the walls between heart chambers. Some defects can be corrected by surgery.

CORONARY HEART DISEASE

Coronary heart disease results from a restricted supply of blood to the heart muscle. When arteries become clogged, or narrowed, by deposits of hardened fat, cholesterol, and other substances called plaque, blood does not flow through them easily. The most common type of heart attack is caused by a blockage of one of the coronary (heart) arteries by a blood clot (thrombosis) that cuts off the blood supply to the region of the heart served by that artery. This damages or kills the deprived tissue, and the injury is called a *myocardial infarction. Angina* is not a disease in its own right but is the name for pain that occurs when the muscular wall of the heart becomes temporarily short of oxygen.

Myocardial infarction is the leading cause of death for adults in the United States. Each year, 1.5 million Americans have a heart attack and one-third of these people die. Some factors that predispose people to heart attacks cannot be modified: family history of heart disease, growing older, and being male. But there are other risks that can be reduced or eliminated: cigarette smoking, high blood cholesterol, high blood pressure, obesity, diet high in saturated fats, and lack of exercise. By not smoking, eating a healthful diet, exercising regularly, and treating their high blood pressure, many people can avoid having heart attacks.

Symptoms of a heart attack vary, but the most common is a persistent, crushing chest pain that may spread to the left arm, jaw, neck, or shoulder blades and last as long as twelve hours. Sometimes a heart attack causes just a mild pain that can be mistaken for indigestion, but indigestion can usually be relieved by antacids. Some people have a feeling of im-

Thirty-year-old Jake suddenly felt a tightening in his chest. The pain and pressure became stronger. He wondered if he had indigestion. But the pain persisted for several minutes and spread to his shoulders and arms on both sides, as well as to the back of his neck. Jake had studied the symptoms of heart attack and knew if there was some question about it he should call 911. The operator asked if he had nausea, cold sweats, vomiting, or other symptoms. He did not, but these do not always accompany a heart attack. Since early treatment is important, an ambulance was sent to Jake's house immediately and within fifteen minutes he was in the hospital. There, an electrocardiogram showed he was having a heart attack. The cardiology team was mobilized and X rays were taken of the arteries leading to his heart to tell if there was a blockage. In less than an hour, an artery was opened and a small stainless steel coil, called a stent, was placed at the site of the blockage to prevent it from closing again. In less than two hours after he left home, Jake was moved to intensive care and on the road to recovery.

pending doom, fatigue, nausea, vomiting, shortness of breath, coolness in the arms, anxiety, and restlessness. There are also "silent heart attacks," which cause no symptoms at all. To confirm the diagnosis of a heart attack, doctors listen to the heart; check for abnormalities using an electrocardiogram, an instrument that records electrical activity in the heart; measure an enzyme in the blood; and in some cases order further tests.

Treatment is aimed at preserving the heart tissue, restoring blood flow in the coronary arteries, relieving pain, and making sure that the heart is pumping properly. Early diagnosis of a suspected heart attack is important, because immediate treatment can prevent further damage and save lives. For example, clot-dissolving drugs given within the first two hours can reduce the size of the damaged area. Various drugs are used for the relief of pain, to improve the pumping action of the heart, and to prevent abnormal rhythms. Oxygen is usually given. In some cases, the doctor inserts a tube into the artery in order to widen the narrowed area. In other cases, coronary artery bypass graft surgery is performed, in which arteries from other parts of the body are transplanted to the heart to provide increased blood flow to the heart muscle.

HEART FAILURE

In heart failure, the heart cannot pump enough blood to meet the body's needs. This may be due to heart muscle being weakened by conditions such as high blood pressure, myocardial infarction, or a mechanical failure in the valves. Heart failure does not mean that the heart stops pumping—that's called *cardiac arrest*—but rather that the heart is not working efficiently.

Increased heart rate, abnormal heart rhythm, shortness of breath, cough, fluid buildup in the body leading to swelling of the feet and ankles or abdomen, weakness, and fatigue are some of the signs of heart failure. These vary, depending on the severity of the failure and the part of the heart affected. A variety of drugs can be prescribed to widen blood vessels, prevent the buildup of fluids, and strengthen heart contractions.

HEART RHYTHM DISORDERS

There are special cells in the heart that act as a natural pacemaker, sending electrical signals through their fibers to the heart muscle and regulating the heartbeat. An electrocardiogram reproduces these electrical patterns as a tracing. When there is a disturbance in any part of this conduction system, the heart may beat irregularly, or the rate may become either very slow (*bradycardia*) or very fast (*tachycardia*). Irregular heartbeats (*arrhythmias*) can be life threatening in some cases, because the heart is unable to pump blood efficiently.

Many people with heart rhythm disorders are able to live normal lives because of the invention of the pacemaker. This device is implanted in the body, and it sends electrical signals to the heart to keep the heart beating at a normal rate. Not everyone with heart rhythm disorders needs a pacemaker; some people can be treated with drugs.

HEART VALVE DISORDERS

The heart has four sets of valves that control the flow of blood passing through its four chambers. Most problems are caused by narrowing and obstruction (called stenosis) or incomplete closing (insufficiency). When a valve is defective and does not close completely, blood leaks back. These defects cause the heart to work harder to pump the blood, and can result in heart failure. An abnormality in a valve is usually discovered when the doctor hears a murmur while listening to the heart with a stethoscope. Disorders of the valves may be caused by congenital abnormalities (present at birth) or by infection or inflammation. A heart murmur does not always mean that a person has a serious disease. An estimated 5 percent of adults, mostly women, have a condition known as *mitral valve prolapse,* which causes problems for only a small number of these individuals.

HIGH BLOOD PRESSURE (HYPERTENSION)

Relatively few young people have high blood pressure, but it does run in families and doctors now believe that it has its roots in childhood. For some children, abnormally high blood pressure starts as early as the first year of life, during childhood, or in adolescence. Some studies suggest that limiting salt in the diet may help to prevent it.

Blood pressure is the amount of force exerted by the blood on the artery walls as blood is pumped through the circulatory system from the heart. Low blood pressure is not abnormal, unless it is caused by some condition that makes it drop too much, causing dizziness, fainting, or loss of consciousness.

Half of the people in the United States have high blood pressure by age sixty-five, but some people never develop it. Many, whether young or old, do not even know they have it. Although there are no symptoms—no aches and pains—when high blood pressure is not treated, it increases the risk of heart disease, stroke, and kidney failure.

Blood pressure can be measured with various instruments, and it is recorded in two numbers. The arterial pressure, when the heart beats, is called the systolic pressure, and it is higher than the diastolic pressure, the figure that represents the pressure in the arteries between beats. Although normal pressure for a child is about 105 over 60, normal pressure for adults is about 120 over 80. Blood pressure increases with age in many people. The high normal figures for a healthy person are 140 (systolic) and 90 (diastolic).

Readings vary from arm to arm and from time to time, so several measurements are taken before a decision is made about whether or not blood pressure is elevated or is too low. *White coat hypertension* (a rise due to being anxious when a doctor or nurse takes the reading), stress, the position of the body, and many other factors can alter blood pressure in the short term.

When readings continue to be high, doctors suggest reducing weight and stress, limiting salt and fatty foods in the diet, exercising, not smoking, and limiting the use of alcohol in an effort to keep pressure under control. Heredity, increasing age, and being male are risk factors that cannot be controlled. When steps such as those listed above do not prove successful, drugs are prescribed. Many kinds of prescription drugs are available for those who need to lower their blood pressure. Good health habits need to be continued even when drugs are taken.

MYOCARDITIS AND PERICARDITIS

Myocarditis is an inflammation of the heart muscle, and pericarditis is an inflammation of the pericardium, the membranous bag surrounding the heart. These conditions may be due to rheumatic fever, infection, complications of tuberculosis, cancer, or kidney failure, and a number of other disorders.

RHEUMATIC FEVER AND RHEUMATIC HEART DISEASE

Before the use of antibiotics, rheumatic fever was a widespread problem, one that often caused heart disease in children. It follows a streptococcal infection, usually strep sore throat, and it causes a rash, fever, joint pain, damage to heart valves, and sometimes to other parts of the heart. Fewer than 1 percent of people with strep infection develop rheumatic fever. A child with rheumatic fever is kept on bed rest and may be treated with antibiotics, aspirin, and steroids. Although treatment does not cure the disease or prevent heart inflammation, it suppresses the symptoms. Long-term treatment with antibiotics may prevent later attacks of the disease. However, it is a serious disease that can be prevented by treating strep infections with antibiotics.

2

Disorders of the Digestive System

A hollow tube about twenty-five feet long extends from your mouth to your anus. Wide and bulgy in some places (the stomach and the colon, or large intestine), narrower in other places (the small intestine), looped and draped in the abdomen, this tube is the digestive system, or gastrointestinal tract, and each part has a different function. Digestion begins in the mouth, where food is chewed into smaller pieces and mixed with saliva. When it is swallowed, it passes through the esophagus to the stomach, where it is broken down further by churning and by powerful digestive juices and hydrochloric acid. The stomach empties its contents into the twenty-two-foot-long small intestine, where the digestive process is completed and nutrients are absorbed. Bile, a bitter, greenish liquid from the liver, and enzymes from the pancreas empty into the duodenum (the beginning part of the small intestine) to help digestion. Undigested food, water, and waste are propelled

Digestive System

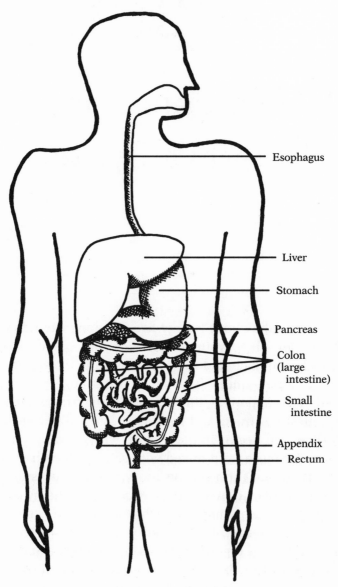

Esophagus

Liver

Stomach

Pancreas

Colon
(large
  intestine)

Small
intestine

Appendix

Rectum

into the large intestine, or colon, where much of the water is reabsorbed. The waste is moved into the rectum and then eliminated through the anus. Usually, your food is digested in this tube without any problems, but sometimes things go wrong. Here are a few of the common disorders of the digestive system.

ABSORPTION DISORDERS

The nutrients from your food are absorbed into your bloodstream mainly in the small intestine. If something interferes with this process, the food is not used properly. Symptoms are diarrhea; fatty, foul-smelling stools; and abdominal pain. This may result in vitamin and mineral deficiencies and anemia, and stunting of growth in children.

Lactose intolerance is caused by a deficiency of lactase, the enzyme necessary to break down lactose, one of the sugars in milk. It is treated by avoiding milk and other foods that contain lactose or by taking lactase tablets. The lactose in yogurt and some kinds of cheese has already been broken down, so these products can usually be eaten without any problems. Babies whose diet consists mainly of milk can be fed soy formula or other milk substitutes.

Another condition that results in problems with absorption is *celiac disease*, an inherited disorder caused by an

You smell a pizza that has just been delivered, and immediately your salivary glands are stimulated. You take a large bite, chew it, and swallow. The swallowed pizza moves through the esophagus, past a muscular band at the end of it, which relaxes to let the food pass into your stomach. Several hours go by before all the pizza gets through your stomach, where it is transformed into a thick, liquid material. From the stomach, partially digested pizza moves into the small intestine, a 22-foot-long, two- to three-inch-wide tube. Here, special secretions complete the breakdown of food into matter that can be absorbed through the lining of the small intestine. Indigestible matter passes into the five-foot-long colon, or large intestine, and is stored in the rectum as feces, then expelled through the anus.

Weiwei came home from a birthday party complaining of a stomachache and diarrhea after eating a large bowl of ice cream and a glass of milk. Her mother was not surprised, because she knew that Weiwei, like most Asians, had a common condition known as lactose intolerance. The condition is most common in Asians, African-Americans, and native Americans, but about 75 percent of all adults except those of northern European heritage show some degree of lactose intolerance.

allergy to gluten, which is a protein found in wheat and rye flour. The lining of the small intestine thins and is unable to absorb nutrients. Diarrhea and bloating begin a few weeks after cereal is introduced into the baby's diet. The infant becomes fretful, fails to thrive, and looks undernourished. Treatment involves avoiding all foods with gluten; these include many processed foods such as soups, hot dogs, and gravies, in addition to breads and cookies made with wheat, rye, and other grains that contain gluten.

Many other conditions (including some kinds of anemia), infections, various drugs, and radiation injury can interfere with the proper absorption of nutrients.

Shauna woke up with vague pain in her abdomen, around her belly button, and she didn't feel hungry for breakfast. She stayed in bed, but the pain got worse and it moved to the lower right side of her abdomen. Then she started feeling nauseated, and she vomited twice. When Shauna's mother took her to the doctor, he examined her, did a blood test, and said that she probably did not have just an ordinary stomachache or intestinal upset. He suspected appendicitis, and Shauna might need surgery.

APPENDICITIS

The appendix is a narrow, fingerlike tube with a closed end. It is about three or four inches long and extends from the cecum, the beginning of the large intestine (colon). Its function is not known. Sometimes it gets obstructed by fecal material, or its lining becomes ulcerated. When this happens, infection sets in and the appendix becomes inflamed and full of pus. The treatment for appendicitis is appendectomy—surgical removal of the appendix. If it is not treated, the appendix ruptures and the infection spreads into the abdominal cavity, causing serious problems. Appendicitis may mimic any of a large number of conditions that cause abdominal pain. Laxatives and enemas should never be given to anyone with abdominal pain because they may cause an infected appendix to burst.

CONSTIPATION

Constipation is the condition of infrequent and difficult passage of hard stools. The term has different meanings for different people. Some think that they must have a bowel movement every day, but many healthy, normal people have only two or three bowel movements a week. Change in routine, stress, traveling, lack of exercise, lack of fiber in the diet, insufficient amount of liquid, and certain medications can all cause constipation. Constipation can be controlled by eating a high-fiber diet containing fruits, vegetables, and whole grains; by drinking six to eight glasses of water or other liquids every day; and by keeping regular bowel habits. High-fiber preparations such as Metamucil are also useful. Laxatives should be used only when needed on occasion, and never regularly, because they disrupt normal functioning and promote dependence on them. In some instances, constipation may be a sign of a tumor of the colon or other serious problem, but this is not generally the case. However, any persistent change in bowel habits is a signal to consult your doctor.

DIARRHEA

Diarrhea is the frequent passage of loose, watery stools, sometimes accompanied by cramps. Like constipation, it is

not a disease but a symptom. It may be due to an infection of the digestive system—viral, bacterial, or parasitic. Eating contaminated food is a common cause, and many people become ill when they travel to places where the sanitation is poor. Most mild cases of diarrhea that are not accompanied by fever or bloody stools subside in a few days on their own. Nonprescription medications are helpful, as are soft foods and adequate replacement of fluids to prevent dehydration. Disorders such as colitis (inflammation of the colon), irritable bowel syndrome, tumors, and pancreatitis may cause diarrhea. (See discussions of irritable bowel syndrome and pancreatitis later in this chapter.) It can also be caused by certain medications. Vomiting, high fever, blood in the stools, and diarrhea that lasts for more than a few days are signs that a doctor should be consulted. When infants have diarrhea, it may be life threatening, for they become dehydrated rapidly.

DIVERTICULOSIS

Diverticula are small balloonlike sacs, usually about one-fourth to one-half inch long. They are outpouchings of the large intestine (colon) in places where the wall has become weakened. Diverticulosis is the name given to the disorder characterized by the presence of diverticula. About two-thirds of all Americans have diverticulosis by age sixty, but most people don't know they have it, for there are no symptoms unless the sacs become inflamed. The condition is then known as *diverticulitis;* the *itis* at the end means "inflammation." The inflammation causes abdominal pain, diarrhea or constipation, and sometimes bleeding.

Researchers have found that diverticula are more common in people who live in Western, industrialized societies and eat low-fiber, highly processed foods, but rare in people who consume high-fiber diets. The outpouchings are thought to be the result of increased pressure in the colon produced by hard, compacted stools. A high-fiber diet or a high-fiber preparation like Metamucil produces bulkier, softer stools that can be propelled through the colon with less pressure.

HEARTBURN AND INDIGESTION

Heartburn is a burning sensation that is felt behind the breastbone, sometimes extending to the throat or jaw, but it has nothing to do with the heart. It is sometimes due to a weakness of the muscular valve between the esophagus and stomach, which allows a backflow of acid from the stomach into the esophagus. Some foods may also cause heartburn. Avoiding foods that disagree with you, not lying down directly after a meal, and sleeping with your upper body slightly elevated are ways of avoiding heartburn. Antacid medication neutralizes the acid and usually relieves heartburn. There are also drugs that prevent acid secretion. If heartburn is frequent or severe, a physician should be seen, because the esophagus may eventually be damaged by the acid.

Indigestion refers to stomach discomfort or a stomachache, and it includes such symptoms as pain, bloating, belching, nausea, and vomiting. Bloating is usually the result of swallowing large amounts of air. Although it can be the result of a specific disorder or disease, the occasional bout of indigestion is usually short-lived and has no obvious cause.

HEMORRHOIDS (PILES)

Hemorrhoids are swollen veins in the area of the rectum and anus. Symptoms include bleeding, pain, burning, and itching. They are very common in people over the age of forty in the United States and other Western countries. The condition is rare in places where the diet contains few processed foods and more fiber. Hemorrhoids are caused by excessive pressure in the veins, often due to constipation, obesity, or pregnancy.

Treatment consists of changing the diet to include more fruits and vegetables, whole grains, and beans, in addition to using ointments for temporary relief. In most cases, symptoms can be controlled with these simple measures. Occasionally, the tissue must be removed surgically or treated by other methods, such as freezing, tying off, injecting the veins with a special chemical, or treating them with lasers, to shrink and close them down. Although bright red blood in the stools may be due to hemorrhoids, sometimes it's a sign of a more serious condition, so blood in the stools should always be checked by a doctor.

INFLAMMATORY BOWEL DISEASE

This term refers to chronic inflammatory diseases of the intestine of unknown cause, mainly Crohn's disease and ulcerative colitis.

Crohn's disease affects the last part of the small intestine and generally part of the colon as well. It seems to run in families and is more common among Jews of European descent. Crohn's disease is often very distressing and difficult to deal with, for it causes weight loss, diarrhea, loss of appetite, fever, abdominal pain, and deterioration of health in general. The first bout of the disease usually occurs during early adulthood, and additional episodes are likely to follow. Although there is no known cure, various medications are used to keep it in check. Corticosteroid drugs reduce the inflammation, antibiotics are used for infection, and other medications are given to control pain and diarrhea. Surgery is not a cure but is sometimes necessary to remove severely diseased parts of the intestine. Although attacks almost always recur, many people enjoy years of good health free of symptoms.

Ulcerative colitis is more common than Crohn's disease; inflammation is usually limited to the colon. The main symptoms are rectal bleeding, diarrhea, abdominal pain, weight loss, and fever. Although sometimes the entire colon is involved, in most cases only the lower part is affected. Treatment is similar to that for Crohn's disease. In severe cases that do not respond to medical treatment, surgery is necessary to remove the diseased part of the colon. People who have had ulcerative colitis for many years appear to have an increased risk for colon cancer. (See discussion of colon cancer in chapter 14.)

IRRITABLE BOWEL SYNDROME (IBS OR SPASTIC COLON)

This syndrome is caused by excessive contractions of the colon, which cause cramping pain or discomfort and alterations in bowel habits, such as episodes of diarrhea and/or constipation. It is the most common gastrointestinal disorder in Western society. No one knows what causes it, but stress and diet may be triggers in some instances. Although the symptoms may resemble those of colitis or other diseases, IBS is a very different disorder; the colon is normal except for its excessive contractions. Other, more serious conditions must be ruled out before the diagnosis of IBS is made. A high-fiber diet and occasional use of medication to slow the intestinal activity are often helpful in treating the symptoms.

NAUSEA AND VOMITING

Everyone has probably experienced nausea and vomiting at some time. Vomiting is a reflex action that is controlled by a special area of the brain. It can be triggered by many different conditions, such as food poisoning, motion sickness, emotional upset, infections, liver disease, and pregnancy. If the nausea and vomiting last for only a short time and can be linked to a likely cause—motion sickness, for example— and if they are not accompanied by other symptoms, there is usually no reason for concern. Prolonged vomiting can be dangerous, however, because dehydration may result, and the body's chemical balance may be disturbed. Bleeding is another danger sign. If vomit contains blood or is stained with green bile, you should see your doctor.

PANCREATITIS

The pancreas is a gland that serves two functions. It secretes the hormone insulin, which is necessary for the metabolism of sugar. (See chapter 10, "Hormonal Disorders.") It also secretes digestive enzymes that are needed to break down proteins, fats, and carbohydrates into substances that can be absorbed in the small intestine. A duct leads from the pancreas to the duodenum, entering the intestine near the bile duct leading from the gallbladder.

Sometimes the pancreatic enzymes are activated prematurely and they digest some of the pancreas itself. The resulting inflammation is called pancreatitis. No one knows exactly why it happens, but pancreatitis is often associated with gallstones or alcoholism. Sometimes it is a complication of injury, surgery, or infection. An acute attack is usually marked by sudden onset of severe, steady pain in the abdomen, which sometimes goes to the back; vomiting; cold, clammy skin; lowered blood pressure; and fast pulse. Pancreatitis can be diagnosed by testing for amylase, a pancreatic enzyme that is present in large amounts in the blood and urine of an individual with pancreatitis.

Treatment consists of giving medication for pain and providing fluids through a vein. Occasionally, individuals suffer from milder attacks over a period of years, and the pancreas gradually becomes damaged and can no longer produce adequate amounts of the enzymes needed for digestion. Pancreatic enzyme supplements can help digestion in such cases. If abdominal pain is due to a blocked duct, surgery to allow drainage may be indicated.

POLYPS

Polyps are small mushroomlike growths of the lining of the intestine protruding into the colon, and they are common in people over the age of forty. There are several syndromes in which there is an inherited tendency for developing multiple polyps, often at an early age. These growths that occur in the colon may not cause any symptoms, except for bleeding. Bleeding may be so slight that it is not noticed unless a special stool test is done to detect signs of blood. It is important to discover the presence of polyps because they tend to become cancerous. Although small polyps are usually not malignant in the beginning, as they grow larger, the potential for becoming cancerous increases. For this reason, doctors recommend their removal. (See discussion of colon cancer in chapter 14.)

ULCER

Peptic ulcer is a common disorder, causing various symptoms such as abdominal pain, heartburn, nausea, vomiting, loss of appetite, and bloating. A peptic ulcer is a sore or crater in the lining membrane (usually in the stomach or duodenum) that extends down into the underlying muscle layer. Although doctors believed for many years that excess stomach acid and pepsin (a digestive enzyme) were responsible for causing ulcers, in the 1980s researchers discovered that a bacterium known as *H. pylori* is responsible for most ulcers. Acid, aspirin and other medications, cigarettes, alcohol, and stress can all make ulcer symptoms worse, but they are not the main cause. Contrary to myth, spicy foods do not cause ulcers, and drinking milk does not help heal them. In fact, milk increases the production of acid. Doctors now recommend that people should eat what they like and avoid any specific foods that disagree with them.

Several kinds of drugs are used in the treatment of ulcers: antacids, which neutralize stomach acid; blocking agents, which lower the production of acid; and protective agents, which form a coating over the ulcer to help it heal. Adding an antibiotic is an important new treatment because it kills the ulcer-causing bacteria and shortens recovery time. Most people with ulcers recover with medication, but sometimes surgery is necessary if there is massive bleeding or if the ulcer penetrates so deeply that the intestine or stomach becomes perforated.

Disorders of the Liver

The liver is one of the largest organs in the body. It is situated on the upper right side of the abdomen, just under the diaphragm, which is the large muscle that separates the chest from the abdomen. It is a complicated organ and performs hundreds of tasks necessary for the functioning of the body. Here are four of its important functions: (1) It produces numerous essential compounds, such as bile, cholesterol, enzymes, and many other proteins. (2) It breaks down and detoxifies many substances, including alcohol and drugs. (3) It controls the levels of blood sugar and fats. (4) It acts as a storehouse for certain substances such as glycogen, which is transformed to glucose when the body needs it. The liver has a remarkable ability to regenerate its own damaged tissue, but despite this ability, there are numerous disorders that can affect its functioning.

CIRRHOSIS

Cirrhosis may be the end result of various kinds of inflammation of the liver, such as that due to chronic viral hepatitis, congenital disease, toxic chemicals ingested, breathed, or absorbed through the skin, and a number of other liver disorders. But alcoholism is the most common cause of cirrhosis in the United States. It is estimated that 15 to 20 percent of heavy drinkers have some degree of cirrhosis. Most cases are found in people between the ages of forty and fifty-five, but cirrhosis can occur even in much younger individuals.

Unlike many diseases that cannot be controlled because scientists have not yet discovered a cause or cure, liver disease from excessive alcohol consumption is an example of a condition that can be prevented. Many people do not realize that alcohol is a poison and is toxic to liver tissue. When it is consumed in large amounts over a period of time, it causes deposits of fat in liver cells, inflammation, liver enlargement, and eventual destruction of liver cells, which are replaced by scar tissue. If the person stops drinking and the cirrhosis is not too advanced, the liver can repair itself and can still carry on its functions. But if the destruction (from continued drinking or from other causes of cirrhosis) continues, the liver becomes scarred, fibrous, and shrunken, no longer able to carry on its vital functions, and every system in the body is affected. Toxic substances build up in the body; proteins, fats, and sugars are not broken down and utilized properly; and many other biochemical processes are disrupted. Here are a few of the many consequences: weakness, swelling of the abdomen due to fluid accumulation, hormonal imbalances, kidney failure, anemia, blood-clotting abnormalities, brain and nervous-system damage, and eventual coma and death.

Another danger that may accompany cirrhosis is life-threatening gastrointestinal bleeding. Severe scarring of liver tissue prevents normal blood circulation, so new blood vessels grow around the stomach and lower esophagus.

Sometimes massive hemorrhage from these veins occurs, and the individual may bleed to death.

Liver transplants can save the lives of people who have certain kinds of liver disease such as some inherited disorders and some cases of cirrhosis.

GALLSTONES

The liver produces a greenish liquid called bile, which flows into a small sac, the gallbladder, where it is stored. From there it is released through a duct into the upper part of the small intestine, the duodenum, where it is used for digesting fats. Sometimes stones form in the gallbladder from elements in the bile. Many older people have gallstones, and although most never have any symptoms, some experience attacks of pain, bloating, and "indigestion" often triggered by eating fatty meals or drinking alcohol. An attack occurs when a stone blocks the duct; the gallbladder becomes stretched, causing pain in the upper part of the abdomen that sometimes extends to the back or right shoulder blade. The pain subsides when the stone passes through the duct into the small intestine. When the blockage persists, severe pain, inflammation of the gallbladder (known as *cholecystitis*), infection, liver damage, and jaundice may occur. (Jaundice is a condition that turns the skin and eyes a yellowish hue, the result of excess bile pigment in the blood.) Surgery to remove the gallbladder (cholecystectomy) is considered the best treatment for cholecystitis and for gallstones, but not everyone needs surgery. People who experience infrequent, mild attacks are sometimes treated by changing their diet, by taking drugs to dissolve the stones, or with the use of a special tube through which the stones can be located and removed, or an obstruction relieved.

HEPATITIS

Fiona returned to school feeling healthy and full of energy after a summer at camp. But about a month later, she woke up one morning with a fever and headache. She had no appetite, and she was very tired. At first she thought she had the flu, but she didn't get better, and she felt exhausted after the slightest effort, no matter how much she slept. When the doctor examined Fiona, she found that the whites of Fiona's eyes and her skin had a yellowish tinge. This yellowish coloration is called jaundice, and it is caused by an excessive amount of bile pigments in the tissues. These pigments are produced by the liver when it breaks down red blood cells. Liver infection is only one of a number of disorders that may cause jaundice. Fiona's liver was enlarged, and it felt sore when the doctor pressed on her belly. A test of her blood confirmed the doctor's diagnosis of viral hepatitis, a liver infection. Fiona learned that several of her fellow campers had also become ill with hepatitis. The infection was traced to a cook at the camp who hadn't washed his hands when preparing food.

Hepatitis, or inflammation of the liver, may be the result of drugs, alcohol, or infection by bacteria, parasites, fungi, or viruses. Most hepatitis is caused by viruses. *Hepatitis A* virus is transmitted by food, water, and eating utensils contaminated with fecal material. The virus is shed from the intestinal tract, and infected people may spread it by handling food with unwashed hands. Eating raw shellfish from water contaminated with sewage is another common source of infection.

The other common form of viral hepatitis, *hepatitis B*, also known as *serum hepatitis*, is transmitted by contaminated blood, sexual contact with an infected partner, or contaminated needles. Hepatitis B is more serious than A; some people develop liver cancer or cirrhosis (irreversible destruction of the liver). (See discussion of cirrhosis on pages 25–27.) *Hepatitis C*, formerly rare, is becoming more common. Many recovered patients become carriers of the virus. Therefore, people who have had hepatitis B or C should not donate blood.

Treatment of hepatitis consists of rest, low-fat diet, and no alcohol or other drugs that might affect the liver. It takes several months for the liver to repair itself, but most people recover completely, and they develop antibodies that give them permanent immunity to the virus.

Vaccines are available for immunization against hepatitis A and B. Gamma globulin injections (containing antibodies to hepatitis) also give protection, but only for a short period of time. Gamma globulin gives immediate protection to people who have not been immunized. It takes several months after vaccination for a person to build up his or her own protective antibodies.

4

Disorders of the Kidney

Just above your waist, at the back of your abdomen on either side of your spinal column, lies a pair of bean-shaped organs that are so important that the heart pumps more blood to them than to any other organ—about one and one-half quarts a minute. These organs are the kidneys, and they are responsible for keeping all your body cells bathed in fluid that is much like the sea where the first one-celled animals evolved. In the kidneys, a huge number of tiny units (called glomeruli) made up of specialized cells constantly filter an enormous amount of water and salts from the blood through a network of tiny, thin-walled blood vessels. This fluid passes into tiny tubes, where most of the water is reabsorbed. The kidneys regulate the amount of water, nutrients, and salts so that a precise balance is maintained in the body fluids. Waste products and excess water are filtered out in this process and eliminated as urine. The urine flows into the bladder from the kidneys through narrow tubes called the ureters. From the bladder, urine is passed through the urethra to the outside. In addition to maintaining the body's chemical balance and removing

Urinary System

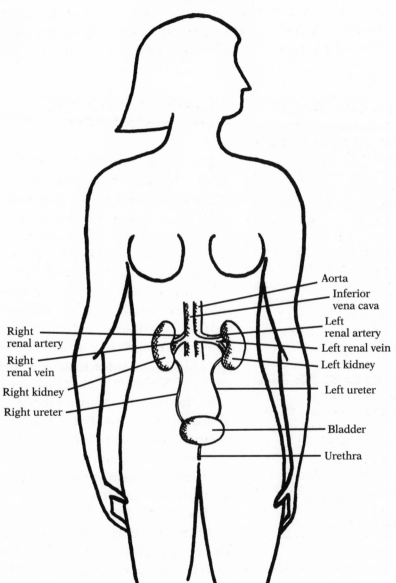

Aorta

Inferior
vena cava

Left
renal artery

Left renal vein

Left kidney

Left ureter

Bladder

Urethra

Right
renal artery

Right
renal vein

Right kidney

Right ureter

wastes, the kidneys perform other functions, such as helping to regulate blood pressure. Infections, congenital disorders, toxins, tumors, and disease in other body systems may affect the kidneys. The following are a few examples.

Eight-year-old Casey woke up with a bad sore throat one morning, but he soon felt better and went back to school after a few days. Two weeks later, he noticed that his urine had a very dark color. He felt nauseated and ill, he had a bad headache, and his face was swollen and puffy. The doctor said that Casey had post-streptococcal glomerulonephritis (PSGN). This is an inflammation of the kidneys that sometimes occurs after a strep infection of the throat.

The dark color of Casey's urine was caused by blood cells that leaked through the walls of injured blood vessels in the glomeruli. His body tissues swelled because the damaged kidney cells could not remove the proper amounts of salt and water. Fortunately, like most children with PSGN Casey recovered completely.

INFLAMMATION OF THE KIDNEYS (NEPHRITIS)

Nephritis is a general term that means kidney inflammation, and its causes are numerous. Infectious organisms such as strep and other bacteria, viruses, fungi, and parasites may be responsible. In addition, many drugs and other substances, including heroin and lead, are toxic to the kidneys. Certain conditions or disease elsewhere in the body can also affect the kidneys. In some instances, the cause of nephritis cannot be found.

In the case of poststreptococcal glomerulonephritis (PSGN), the nephritis is not due to a direct infection of the kidney cells by the invading organism, but is caused by an immune reaction to the germ. No bacteria are found in the kidney or in the urine as is the case with kidney infection (see page 34). Antigens (protein substances) in the strep bacteria provoke the person's immune system to manufacture antibodies. Kidney damage is the result of the chemical compounds formed by this reaction. Although strep infection is the most common cause of this kind of nephritis, other organisms may sometimes induce it.

PSGN was more common before the discovery of penicillin and other antibiotics that are now used to fight bacterial infections. Antibiotics do not cure PSGN after it develops, but when they are used to treat strep throat, PSGN can be prevented. There is no specific treatment for PSGN. However, in some cases, salt intake may be restricted, or diuretics may be used to rid the body of excess fluid.

KIDNEY FAILURE

The end result of many kidney disorders is kidney failure. As kidney damage progresses, fluid and chemical balance are disturbed, and toxic substances build up in the body. Symptoms may include fatigue, nervous system abnormalities such as decreased mental functioning, nausea, vomiting, wasting of the body, itching, high blood pressure, heart failure, anemia, and bleeding.

Many people who died of kidney failure in the past could have had their lives prolonged or saved by the improved treatments available today. Approximately 100,000 people in the United States are currently being kept alive by dialysis machines, which function as artificial kidneys. Invented in 1946, the dialysis machine works as follows: The person's blood is pumped from a vein through tubing into the machine, which filters out the wastes, and then is returned to the body again. People on dialysis need to spend from four to six hours three times a week connected to the machine. The artificial kidney machine cannot perform the many other important functions of normal kidneys, so it does not relieve all the complications of kidney failure. For example, anemia, bleeding, weakness, high blood pressure, and infections may continue to plague the person. Despite these problems, many people are able to continue leading productive lives for a long time.

Kidney transplantation, first performed in 1954, has also enabled more people to live longer. The success rate of the operation has increased as researchers have learned more about the immune system and how to prevent the recipient's body from rejecting the donated kidney.

KIDNEY INFECTIONS (PYELONEPHRITIS)

Bacteria from outside the body can travel up the urethra to the bladder, and from there to the kidneys, causing infection. Symptoms include flank pain, chills, fever, and frequency of urination. Obstruction of the urinary tract—for example an enlarged prostate constricting the urethra—predisposes an individual to infection. Sometimes, only the bladder is involved; but all urinary tract infections should be treated with appropriate antibiotics prescribed by a doctor, as they may progress slowly and unnoticed and lead to severe kidney damage and eventual failure.

Kidney infection, or pyelonephritis, is diagnosed by taking a urine specimen and testing it to see if bacteria is present.

NEPHROSIS (NEPHROTIC SYNDROME)

Nephrosis refers to a group of symptoms often found in people who have kidney diseases. It is also seen in individuals who do not have nephritis or other disease. In nephrosis, the filtering membrane does not function normally, allowing proteins to leak from the blood into the urine. Fluid is retained in the body tissues and causes swelling of the face, abdomen, hands, and feet. Nephrosis can cause malnutrition (due to loss of protein) and other complications such as blood clots.

Nephrosis is most common in young children, and in most of these cases, no cause can be found and there is no damage to the kidney tissues. Almost all cases are completely cured by treatment with steroids.

OTHER KIDNEY PROBLEMS

Some older people develop *stones* in their kidneys, which may cause excruciating pain or blockage of the ureters and infection unless they are small enough to be passed in the urine. Some kinds of stones are due to a birth defect known as cystinuria; this causes changes in the chemical composition of the urine, and stones are formed.

There are many other inherited kidney diseases or conditions. For example, some people are born with only *one kidney* and never realize it. A rare inherited disorder, called *polycystic kidneys,* marked by the presence of many cysts (fluid-filled sacs) in the kidneys at birth, results in kidney failure at an early age, often before adolescence.

5

Disorders of the Eyes

Vision is the most complex of the senses and the most specialized. Light rays enter the pupil and register on the retina at the back of the eyeball. Here, images are translated into electrical impulses that are carried to the brain, where we recognize what we see. The chamber in front of the iris (the colored part of the eye) is filled with a fluid called aqueous humor, and the back cavity is filled with a clear gel called vitreous humor.

Eyes are surprisingly tough, but they can be affected by a wide variety of diseases. Some of the most common occur when people are old, but even young children can suffer from some kinds of eye disease.

CATARACT

A cataract is an opaque area in the normally clear lens of the eye. Cataracts occur in many people who are over the age of sixty. They cause no pain, and at first they do not interfere with vision. As the cataracts progress, they cloud the lens of the eye and gradually make the lens opaque. They can be removed and an artificial replacement lens can be substituted to restore vision.

CONJUNCTIVITIS (PINK EYE)

Conjunctivitis is an inflammation of the transparent membrane that lines the eyelid and eyeball up to the margin of the cornea (the layer of clear tissue with an overlying film of tears at the front of the eye). Conjunctivitis is common among children, and when caused by bacteria it is extremely contagious. When allergies are the cause it is not infectious, but an immune response of your body to ward off what it perceives as an invader. Although conjunctivitis is usually harmless to sight, it should be diagnosed and treated by a doctor because it may spread and cause complications if not treated early.

GLAUCOMA

Glaucoma, an eye disease in older people, is characterized by increased pressure in the aqueous humor. The pressure results from faults in the drainage channel between the back of the cornea and the iris. Medication given in eyedrops usually helps to lower the pressure, but surgery may be needed to open a blocked channel or create an artificial one. If left untreated, glaucoma causes permanent loss of vision.

MACULAR DEGENERATION

Macular degeneration is the most frequent cause of legal blindness in the United States. It most frequently affects the elderly. A damaged or diseased macula, an area in the central portion of the retina, causes difficulty in seeing fine print, distant objects, and central vision. Side vision is retained. Early diagnosis is important for successful treatment, so people over fifty are wise to have annual eye examinations to detect this or other eye diseases.

STY

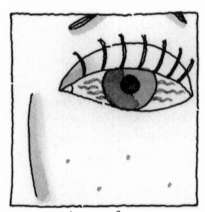

A sty is an infection near the root of an eyelash. It usually develops slowly, forming a painful lump that eventually fills with pus and bursts. The sac should not be squeezed but should be allowed to burst on its own. Antibiotic ointment and warm compresses applied to the eye four times a day usually control the infection. If sties are frequent or stubborn, see your physician.

6

Disorders of the Ears, Nose, and Throat

Your ear serves two functions, hearing and balance, and it consists of three parts: the outer ear, the middle ear, and the inner ear. The outer ear includes the ear canal leading to the eardrum, a thin membrane separating the outer ear from the middle ear. The middle ear is a small cavity containing three tiny bones. A structure called the eustachian tube leads from the throat area behind your nose (the nasopharynx) to the middle ear (the part of the ear behind your eardrum). The eustachian tube equalizes the outside air pressure with the pressure inside the eardrum. The inner ear contains two structures, one called the labyrinth, which affects balance, and the other the cochlea, which affects hearing. Sound waves are funneled into the auditory canal and hit the eardrum, making it vibrate; these vibrations pass through the bones of the middle ear and then to the cochlea. Impulses from the cochlea travel to the brain along the auditory nerve. These impulses are then interpreted by your brain as musical sounds, speech, running water, etc.

The nose is the entrance to the respiratory system; air is breathed in, filtered, and warmed as it goes through the nasal passage down into the throat and then into the trachea on its way to the lungs. (See chapter 7, "Disorders of the Lungs.") The nasal passage is connected to your sinuses, which are air spaces in the bones above and behind your nose.

The throat, or pharynx, is the area at the back of your mouth that leads to the trachea and the esophagus. The voice box, or larynx, is at the top of the trachea. Sounds are produced by the air passing over the vocal cords in the larynx.

BLOCKED TUBES

If you have ever flown in an airplane when your nose has been stuffed (and your eustachian tubes blocked) because of a cold, you may have experienced ear pain and some loss of hearing during the descent before landing. This occurs because the air pressure in the cabin increases, but your blocked eustachian tubes do not allow the air through to your middle ear. This creates a greater air pressure on the outside of your eardrums than on the inside, and the eardrums are pushed in, causing pain. Taking decongestants before your trip, sucking candy, chewing gum, and swallowing frequently can help this condition.

COMMON COLD

When you wake up with a sore throat and the shivers, it's probably the beginning of a disease that is the most common of all: a cold. Although colds are common, not all colds are the same. There are between 100 and 200 kinds of colds, and immunity against one does not apply to the others.

Cold viruses invade cells that line the throat and nose, where they multiply rapidly. White blood cells attack the viruses, nasal tissues swell, and the secretion of excess mucus results in a runny nose. Certain white blood cells, phagocytes, can engulf and destroy dead and immobilized viruses and damaged cells.

Exposure to cold weather, drafts, and dampness, having wet feet, wet hair, or wet clothing do not cause colds. Some environmental stress may weaken the immune system, but colds are caused by viruses.

Some of the ways to prevent spreading your cold to others are well known. They include covering your mouth when you cough and sneeze, throwing away tissues after use, and avoiding close contact with other people. Washing your hands frequently is especially important since there is evidence that colds can be spread through shaking hands and other touches.

To fight your cold, drink fluids, rest, and eat plenty of fruits and vegetables. Antibiotics can help to prevent other infections that may accompany a cold, but they will not kill the viruses that cause colds. With evidence that germs are becoming increasingly resistant to antibiotics because of their frequent use, doctors avoid prescribing antibiotics to treat colds.

Colds and other nasal infections sometimes lead to *in-*

flammation and infection of the sinuses, causing headache and feelings of being very stuffed up. Using a vaporizer and decongestants often helps, but sometimes antibiotics are needed.

Anosmia, or loss of the sense of smell and taste, is usually due to a cold or allergies. In rare instances, it is caused by a tumor or injury to the olfactory nerve.

HEARING LOSS

Hearing loss is a common problem in older people, because of loss of certain cells in the cochlea during aging, but it can happen to young people, too. One important cause is overexposure to loud noise for long periods of time. Jet engine noise, heavy construction equipment (such as trucks and tractors), jackhammers, and typical rock music concerts can all cause irreversible damage to the sensitive cells of the cochlea. Many rock musicians have noise-induced hearing loss. In this type of hearing loss, called *sensorineural,* the loss is due to nerve failure, and hearing cannot be regained. Sounds can be transmitted to the inner ear, but they do not reach the brain. If you hear noise that causes pain or ringing in your ears, it is probably loud enough to cause nerve damage, possibly permanent. People exposed to noisy machinery should use ear protectors.

Hearing loss may also occur when sounds are prevented from being transmitted to the inner ear. This type of impairment is called *conductive* and can be caused by a condition as simple as an accumulation of wax in the ear canal. Infections, certain medications, head injury, brain tumors, hardening of the arteries, inborn disorders, and neurological diseases are a few of the other conditions that may cause hearing loss.

LARYNGITIS

Laryngitis is an inflammation of the voice box. It is accompanied by such symptoms as dryness and soreness of the throat, hoarseness, cough, and difficulty in swallowing. Laryngitis may be caused by an infection, but sometimes it is due to overuse (e.g., excessive shouting, singing, or talking).

MENIERE'S DISEASE

A serious and debilitating condition, Meniere's disease causes dizziness, hearing loss, and ringing in the ears. It results from an increased amount of fluid in the labyrinth of the ear. No one knows exactly what the underlying cause is, or what triggers the attacks. Allergies, nervous system dysfunction, or increased premenstrual water retention may be responsible in some cases. The person may experience several attacks a year, with no problems in between attacks. Over time, the hearing loss may get worse and may become permanent. The dizziness during attacks may be so bad that the person cannot keep his or her balance and may be forced to stay in bed. In most people, the disorder goes away by itself. In more severe cases, treatment with medication may be necessary, but it is not always effective in preventing attacks. A number of operations have been advocated to treat Meniere's disease, but surgery is usually a last resort.

MIDDLE EAR INFECTION (OTITIS MEDIA)

Middle ear infections are very common in children, especially when they have colds or other respiratory infections.

Verna woke up from her nap in a cranky mood and would not stop crying. She kept rubbing her left ear, and she did not seem interested in her supper. She was only eight months old, so she could not tell her mother what was wrong, but her mother suspected an ear infection. Verna's doctor confirmed the diagnosis and prescribed a course of antibiotics, which cleared up the infection in a few days.

Viruses or bacteria from the nasopharynx flow back through the eustachian tube to the middle ear, where an infection develops. Young children are more susceptible to middle ear infections because of the shape of their eustachian tubes. A middle ear infection causes severe pain, fever, some hearing loss, and occasionally a bulging eardrum or rupture of the eardrum, with drainage of pus into the ear canal. The infection is treated with antibiotics. Permanent damage and loss of hearing can occur if ear infections are not treated properly.

Some children have frequent infections, and others may have an infection that does not clear up, even with antibiotics. Someone who is prone to ear infections may be treated with tubes in his or her ears. The doctor inserts a tiny plastic tube into the eardrum in order to allow fluid to drain from the middle ear to the outside. This helps to relieve the infection and clear the blockage in the eustachian tube. The plastic tube falls out by itself after several months. In the days before antibiotics, ear infections often spread to surrounding areas such as the mastoid bone behind the ear. The only treatment then was to remove the infected bone surgically.

MOTION SICKNESS

Do you become queasy at the thought of riding the roller coaster at the amusement park? Many people experience nausea, vomiting, headache, and sleepiness in cars, planes, or boats. The symptoms of motion sickness are due to excessive stimulation of receptors in the labyrinth of the inner ear. If you are prone to motion sickness, your physician can prescribe effective medication to prevent it when you travel.

NOSEBLEED

The nosebleed is a common problem. Sometimes it is caused by a blow to the nose, but usually it starts suddenly and spontaneously, often when you have a cold or other condition that dries and injures the delicate membranes lining your nose. In most cases, a nosebleed is not a cause for concern. Very rarely, it is due to a bleeding disorder, which would also cause bleeding in other parts of the body. It is easy to stop a nosebleed. Here's what you need to do: Sit down, lean forward, breathe through your mouth, and place steady pressure with a finger on the side that is bleeding. Hold the finger there for about five or ten minutes. After the bleeding stops, be careful not to dislodge the clot that has formed in your nose, or the bleeding will begin again.

PHARYNGITIS (SORE THROAT)

The most common throat disorder, pharyngitis is usually due to a viral infection. There is no specific treatment for viral infections. The most common bacterial cause is streptococcus, or "strep throat," which is more serious and needs to be treated with antibiotics in order to prevent later complications such as poststreptococcal glomerulonephritis. (See chapter 4, "Disorders of the Kidney.") If your doctor suspects strep infection, she will probably take a throat culture to identify the organism and then prescribe antibiotics.

SWIMMER'S EAR

The outer ear canal may become infected if you've been swimming in polluted water. This infection causes pain and a pussy discharge, and should be treated with antibiotic drops prescribed by a physician.

TONSILLITIS

Tonsillitis, or inflammation of the tonsils, is usually caused by strep infection and is most common in children between the ages of five and ten. The tonsils are small masses of tissue at the back of both sides of the throat; they are large during childhood and tend to shrink during adolescence. They contain white blood cells whose function is to help fight infection that might otherwise spread. Before the use of antibiotics, tonsillitis was a more serious problem, and many children had their tonsils removed surgically. That surgical procedure, known as a tonsillectomy, is now performed only when the infection is chronic, and the child has repeated attacks. Tonsillectomy does not prevent colds, which are caused by viruses.

7

Disorders of the Lungs

A ll the cells in your body need a constant supply of oxygen in order to stay alive, and they get it from the air
that you breathe into your lungs. The air is inhaled through
your nose, then into your windpipe, or trachea. This is the
hard tube you can feel at the front of your neck. Inside your
chest, the trachea divides into two tubes called bronchi, one
going to each lung. In the lungs, the bronchi branch into
smaller tubes known as bronchioles. The bronchioles open
into tiny air sacs called alveoli, which look like bunches of
grapes but are too small to be seen without a microscope.
Oxygen from the air you breathe passes through the walls
of the alveoli into tiny blood vessels in these walls, and from
there it is carried by the blood to other parts of the body.
Carbon dioxide, which is a waste product, is also carried in
the blood, and it passes into the alveoli, where it is exhaled
with the used air.

When you are healthy and your body is functioning normally, you don't think about your respiratory system—all
the structures involved in breathing—because breathing is
automatic. But there are many conditions and diseases that

Lungs

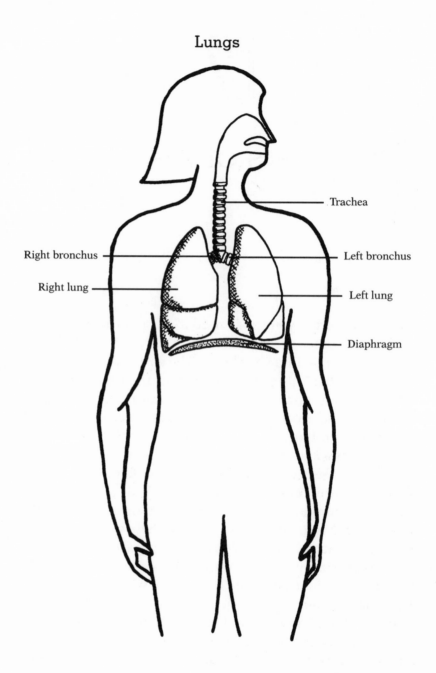

Trachea

Right bronchus

Left bronchus

Right lung

Left lung

Diaphragm

interfere with the normal functioning of this system, including cancer, infections, allergies, inherited disorders, and heart failure. Your lungs may be affected by airborne particles that you inhale, for example, infectious organisms such as bacteria, viruses, and fungi, or irritants like tobacco smoke, asbestos, and coal dust. Many people seek medical attention because they have a cough, chest pain, or difficulty breathing, the most common symptoms of respiratory disease.

ASTHMA

In the United States there are more than 4 million kids under age eighteen who have asthma, and the numbers are rising. Although asthma is a treatable disease, each year more than 5,000 people die from it. It is the leading reason for school absences and for the admission of children to hospitals. Asthma is a disease that makes it difficult for people to breathe at

> In spite of her asthma, Jackie Joyner-Kersee has earned a reputation as the world's best all-around athlete and the greatest heptathlete of all time. She won her first of four consecutive National Pentathlon Championships at the age of fourteen. She went on to win many honors, including Olympic gold medals, and set the world, Olympic, and American records in one single event.

times, because of temporary blockage of the airways when small muscles around the breathing tubes contract abnormally. This causes the wheezing that is the most well-known symptom of asthma. Normally, when a person stops breathing in, the lungs, which are elastic, just relax and let the air out. But people with asthma have trouble breathing out; during an attack, air gets trapped in their lungs because of the blockage, and it feels very uncomfortable to breathe. There are four problems in the airways that cause difficulties with breathing: constriction or narrowing, swelling, inflammation, and too much mucus. People with asthma have supersensitive airways, which tend to over-react by constricting; this tendency is sometimes called twitchiness.

The most common trigger for asthma is allergy. Not everyone with allergies has asthma, but most people with asthma are allergic; pollen, mold, cats and dogs, feathers, and house dust are some of the common offenders. Other triggers of asthma attacks include respiratory infections, cigarette smoke, smog, perfume, certain chemicals added to foods, aspirin, exercise, and cold air.

There are very effective medicines that reduce swelling and twitchiness and open up the narrowed airways so that the person can breathe more easily. Some are taken by mouth and others are inhaled. Although asthma cannot be cured, it can be managed by avoiding known triggers, taking prescribed medications regularly, and watching for trouble signs. If you have asthma, you should know that you can do almost anything that other people can do, even participate in strenuous sports, with guidance from your doctor. Many famous athletes have asthma. (See sidebar.) Kids with asthma should not consider themselves "sick."

BLACK LUNG DISEASE (COAL MINER'S DISEASE)

Black lung disease is caused by inhaling coal dust. It may result in patchy areas of damage to lung tissue that do not necessarily cause problems. But sometimes it progresses to massive damage and formation of scar tissue throughout the lungs, causing severe shortness of breath, coughing, lung infections, and other complications. The risk of developing black lung disease depends partly on how long the person has been exposed to coal dust and the composition of the coal.

Many other kinds of dusts can cause similar lung damage

when they are inhaled. Silica (dust from stone), asbestos, some metal compounds, and certain gases are only a few examples of the hazardous materials that cause disease among workers in certain occupations.

BRONCHITIS

Inflammation of the lining of the bronchi, the main air tubes to the lungs, is known as bronchitis. Almost everyone has had bronchitis on occasion, usually with a cold, if the cold virus attacks the bronchi as well as the nose and throat. The inflammation causes increased production of mucus and cough, which is generally not serious and clears up within a few days if you are a healthy person. However, those who have other lung conditions, those who live in areas of high air pollution, and smokers are more prone to bouts of bronchitis. Some individuals, mainly those who smoke, develop chronic bronchitis; this means that their bronchi are inflamed all the time and constantly produce excessive mucus, causing *smokers' cough*. People with chronic bronchitis are at higher risk for respiratory infections, which cause further damage to the lining of the airways. In some people, the airways become so thickened and narrowed that the flow of air is blocked and breathing becomes difficult. Permanent damage to the airways may be avoided if the person stops smoking in the early stages of bronchitis.

CROUP

Croup is a severe inflammation of the upper airways, usually caused by a viral infection. It generally affects children between the ages of three months and three years. Most

> Two-year-old Zeke had what appeared to be an ordinary cold, but he woke up one night with a sharp, barking cough and noisy breathing; he was gasping and unable to breathe in enough air. Zeke was having an attack of croup.

children can be treated at home—by breathing in steam from a humidifier—but some must be hospitalized and may need oxygen if breathing becomes very difficult.

CYSTIC FIBROSIS

Cystic fibrosis is the most common of the lethal inherited disorders, affecting about 30,000 young people in the United States. Among white children, one baby in every 2,000 births has cystic fibrosis; the figure is much lower for children of color.

Cystic fibrosis kills about half of those who suffer from it by the age of thirty. It affects the lungs, gastrointestinal tract, and pancreas. It causes the breakdown of a system that normally carries salt away from cells that line the intestines, lungs, and some other organs. This leads to the production of sticky, thick mucus, which blocks the airways and lungs, trapping bacteria and causing infection. Repeated bouts of pneumonia and damage to the lungs can eventually lead to death. Pulmonary disease is the main cause of death.

One test for cystic fibrosis is the measurement of salt in sweat, since salt levels are unusually high in those who have this disorder. In addition, a culture of the mucus may reveal bacteria typically found in people with cystic fibrosis.

Although there is no cure for cystic fibrosis, there are a number of treatments that help to prolong life and make sufferers feel more comfortable. One is called postural therapy, in which the person is positioned so that mucus can be drained down. Various medications are given to keep the airways clear. Antibiotics are also used to treat respiratory infections.

A defective gene for cystic fibrosis was discovered in

1989. If both parents carry this defective gene, there is one chance in four that their child will have the disease. In 1992 defective genes were placed in mice, and the mice developed cystic fibrosis. Scientists hope to learn more about treating this disease through the use of mice as models.

EMPHYSEMA

Constant exposure to cigarette smoke may result in permanent damage to the alveolar walls and enlargement of the air sacs. This condition is called emphysema, and it is irreversible. It causes shortness of breath because the normal exchange of oxygen and carbon dioxide is impaired. The combination of chronic bronchitis and emphysema is often referred to as *chronic obstructive pulmonary disease,* or *COPD.* COPD is a leading cause of death in the United States and one of the most disabling conditions that affect older people. You may know someone who coughs and wheezes frequently, and who becomes short of breath climbing stairs or walking fast. On occasion you may have seen older people who have such a severe breathing problem that they must breathe oxygen from a tank that they take wherever they go. Although not all cigarette smokers develop this disease, it is strongly linked to smoking.

LUNG CANCER (SEE CHAPTER 14)

PNEUMONIA (SEE CHAPTER 16)

PULMONARY EDEMA

Certain conditions in other parts of the body cause fluid to build up in the lung tissue, hampering the exchange of oxygen and carbon dioxide in the alveoli. The buildup of fluid is known as edema. Heart disease is a common cause of edema; other conditions include liver disease, some kidney diseases, nutritional deficiencies, and severe burns. People with pulmonary edema suffer from shortness of breath when they exert themselves, attacks of severe breathlessness at night, breathing difficulties when they lie flat, and coughing spells. Edema is treated by trying to correct the disease that caused it, by administering medication that promotes elimination of the excess fluid, and by giving oxygen.

Althea was a normal, active six-month-old baby who seemed to be thriving and healthy. But one morning, her mother found her lying dead in her crib. She had not had a cold or other illness, and there was no sign that she had suffocated in her blanket or choked on vomit. An autopsy did not uncover anything that could have caused her death. Althea's grief-stricken parents felt guilty and blamed themselves for their baby's death, but their doctor assured them that it was not their fault. Althea had died of sudden infant death syndrome, popularly known as SIDS.

SUDDEN INFANT DEATH SYNDROME (SIDS)

Sudden infant death syndrome is among the leading causes of infant death, striking about 8,000 babies in the United States every year. No one knows exactly why it happens, but researchers think that it may be due to an abnormality in the brain center that controls breathing. Doctors have found that placing infants on their backs instead of facedown can reduce the incidence of this problem.

TUBERCULOSIS

Tuberculosis is an infectious disease that attacks the lungs, but it can spread to other organs.

Most of the people who are infected do not develop active

TB—that is, they have no symptoms. People with active TB have such symptoms as a persistent cough and chronic fatigue.

The number of TB cases is on the rise, especially in developing countries. Tuberculosis is not spread easily, but it has infected about half the world's population. Each year, it makes 8 million people sick and kills about 2 to 3 million. Most people who have active TB can be cured by antibiotics. However, millions of people in developing countries do not have access to such drugs. There are increasing numbers of people who have new strains of tuberculosis that are drug resistant.

Tests for tuberculosis are being used more widely in the United States than in the past. This is because travelers and immigrants from developing countries are bringing more cases of TB into the United States. People infected with HIV have weakened immune systems; they have less resistance to other infections and are more likely to acquire TB. In view of the soaring world population that lives largely in crowded conditions, there is an urgent need to step up efforts in the worldwide battle against TB.

Fifteen-year-old Lori was suspected of having tuberculosis of the lungs after she had a positive skin test. X rays showed disease in one lung, and TB germs were found in the mucus she coughed up. She was not worried because she knew she could be cured with antibiotics. She had a persistent cough and she felt rather tired most of the time, but the doctor assured her that she would be fine if she took the antibiotics he prescribed for a year. Lori thought he was kidding about the length of time, but he insisted that she must continue for the full year. After a few months, her cough disappeared, she felt fine, and she stopped taking her medicine.

Soon, Lori's cough came back, so she went to see her doctor again. Tests showed that she now had a more serious kind of tuberculosis, one known as *multidrug resistant TB*, or *MDR-TB*. New strains of bacteria were causing her disease, and they could not be killed by the medicine she had been taking. Lori entered a program in which she reported to a clinic each day and was given special drugs for MDR-TB. She was warned that her disease could become deadly if she did not follow doctor's orders.

8

Disorders of the Nervous System

The brain and the spinal cord are unbelievably complicated. According to the National Institutes of Health,
90 percent of what is known about the brain has been discovered in the last ten years, and a great deal more needs
to be learned. The brain contains as many as 100 billion
cells that make up a complex communication system relay-
ing messages within the brain and between the brain and
the rest of the body. Together with the spinal cord, these
cells control thinking, emotions, behavior, and movement,
and relay sensations from the outside. The brain also controls functions of which you may not always be aware, such
as breathing and swallowing.

Today, death is defined as lack of functioning of the
brain, and not when the heart stops.

Diseases of the brain and other parts of the nervous system include a wide variety of disorders that result in seizures, paralysis, weakness, loss of sensation, and other

serious problems. Some of these diseases are described here.

ALZHEIMER'S DISEASE

Alzheimer's disease has been called the cruelest disease that humans have ever faced, for it gradually destroys the brain. Simple bouts of forgetfulness may be the beginning, but the ending is always the same. The person becomes increasingly confused and helpless. About 4 million people suffer from Alzheimer's in the United States, where it is the fourth leading cause of death among the elderly.

Alzheimer's disease affects the parts of the brain that control thought, memory, and language. Individuals have different symptoms and rates of progress. Several recent genetic discoveries have shed new light on the cause and progress of Alzheimer's disease. Studies about the role of genetic factors may help to identify those at risk for Alzheimer's, especially the kind that develops before the age of sixty-five.

Alzheimer's is not a normal part of aging, and although heredity appears to play a part in some forms of the disease, children and grandchildren of those who suffer from it will not necessarily develop it.

Moira had always enjoyed her grandfather's visits, but recently he seemed different. He could not remember the date of the soccer game, then he forgot the time. Moira even had to help him remember the names of her cousins. His doctor thought he might be in the early stages of Alzheimer's, but there is no test for it. If it turned out that Moira's grandfather in fact had this disease, he would gradually lose all of his mental faculties and would eventually need total care.

Ronald Reagan, the fortieth president of the United States, was inaugurated in 1981. When he began his presidency, he was seventy years old—the oldest president in the nation's history. Five years after finishing his second term, President Reagan wrote a letter to the people of the United States disclosing the fact that his doctors believed he was suffering from Alzheimer's disease.

In addition to plaques and tangles that are found when brains of people with Alzheimer's are autopsied, researchers have found other changes, too. For example, they have noted reduced amounts of certain chemicals that transmit messages from one nerve cell to another. Research is the key to unlocking the mysteries of Alzheimer's disease. Scientists are working toward improved diagnosis and care of those with Alzheimer's as well as trying to find ways to cure and possibly prevent it.

AMYOTROPHIC LATERAL SCLEROSIS (ALS OR LOU GEHRIG'S DISEASE)

As with other diseases, people with ALS come from all walks of life. Some well-known individuals who have been affected by it include:

- Ezzard Charles, heavyweight boxing champion
- Dennis Day, singer
- Lou Gehrig, baseball great
- Stephen Hawking, physicist
- Jacob Javits, U.S. senator
- Charles Mingus, jazz musician
- David Niven, actor
- Eliot Porter, photographer
- Dmitri Shostakovich, composer
- Bob Waters, professional football player
- Charlie Wedemeyer, football coach

People with ALS develop small muscle contractions and weakness and wasting of muscles. This happens when nerve cells (motor neurons) that run from the muscles to the brain stem and spinal cord die. *Amyotrophic* means "lack of nourishment"; *lateral* refers to the nerve *tracts* that run down both sides of the spinal cord, where many of the neurons affected by ALS are found; and *sclerosis*, or hardening, relates to the scar tissue that remains after the nerves have disintegrated. Many people use the term *Lou Gehrig's disease* because ALS first came to the public's attention when the career of Yankee first baseman Lou Gehrig was cut short by it.

ALS can interfere with any part of the body's functioning. The suffering of those who cannot use their arms, cannot swallow, cannot walk or communicate, but whose minds are not impaired has been described as a living death. ALS most commonly strikes men between the ages of forty and seventy. While the mystery about the cause of the disease is lifting, much more needs to be learned before effective treatments are available. Half of ALS patients are dead within three to four years of diagnosis.

CEREBRAL PALSY

Cerebral palsy can happen for a number of reasons. Some include a pregnant woman's use of alcohol and other drugs, German measles during pregnancy, premature birth, lack of oxygen to the central nervous system, and incompatibility between the baby's and the mother's blood. Cerebral palsy can also happen when a baby's brain is damaged due to an accident, an illness such as meningitis, lead poisoning, or repeated beating or shaking of a baby.

Cerebral palsy is the most common cause of crippling in children, occurring in 1.5 to 5 per 1,000 live births. Between 500,000 and 700,000 children and adults in the

Dwayne's cerebral palsy prevented his normal development. He was born prematurely and lived in an incubator for several months. When he came home from the hospital, he needed special care because he had poor muscle control and coordination. He did not learn to crawl until he was three years old. Doctors explained that this was due to damage to the parts of his brain that controlled these functions.

By the time Dwayne was ready for school, he learned to stand with the help of braces, and he was able to travel almost any place he wanted to go in his electric wheelchair. Although he will never be cured, his condition is not expected to get worse. Today, many of his classmates are supportive of his problem and make him feel like part of the group in crafts and other activities.

Dwayne uses special eating utensils and other devices that help him to be fairly independent. His mind is sharp, and he is able to laugh and enjoy life.

Arnie was the star quarterback on the football team, and everyone considered him one of the healthiest people in the senior class. One day in math class, he lost consciousness, fell on the floor, and had a convulsion. His body twitched uncontrollably for several minutes; then he was quiet and seemed dazed. Everyone was very frightened, but the teacher recognized that Arnie was having an epileptic seizure. She assured the class that this would pass and that Arnie would be fine afterward. The school nurse reported the episode to his doctor.

Arnie was as surprised as everyone else to find out that he had epilepsy. He had never had a seizure before, but his doctor explained that epilepsy is not uncommon. About 1 to 2 percent of the population of the United States have this disease, as many as 4 million people.

United States have cerebral palsy, but there is a wide range of impairment. It rarely affects the whole body. In some cases, there is floppiness of the body, and sometimes posture may be twisted. Three main patterns of muscular weakness and spasticity (stiffness of arms and legs) are recognized: all four limbs; arm, leg, and trunk on one side; and both legs. The chest muscles are seldom affected. In some cases, even simple movements, such as reaching for a cup, can be difficult. Many patients are helped by medication, surgery, and occupational and physical therapy.

EPILEPSY

In the past, epileptics were thought to be holy people who communicated with the gods because of their trancelike spells. Epilepsy is still surrounded by myth and misunderstanding, and many epileptics suffer more from the stigma attached to this disorder than from the disease itself. Some people think that epileptics are violent or mentally ill because of their symptoms during a seizure.

Epilepsy, also known as seizure disorder, is a brain condition marked by attacks of abnormal movements, altered consciousness, or unusual behavior. Normally, nerve cells communicate through electrical signals in a controlled, orderly pattern. In an epileptic seizure, the firing of signals between certain cells becomes continuous, very rapid, and uncontrolled. The chaotic electrical activity in the brain may be general, involving wide areas of the brain, or it may be partial, involving only a small area.

In a generalized seizure of the kind that doctors classify as *grand mal,* the person falls down, the body stiffens, and the limbs and body alternately go into spasms and relax. He or she loses consciousness for several minutes, may stop breathing, and sometimes turns bluish. The seizure usually lasts only a few minutes, and the person regains consciousness, but may feel sleepy, confused, and weak for several hours.

Petit mal seizures, or absence seizures, are another kind of generalized seizure, most common in children. They last only a few seconds, and they may occur up to 100 times a day. The attacks may begin with rolling of the eyes and twitching of the mouth. The person stares blankly and appears frozen, but when the seizure ends, resumes what he or she was doing. Absence seizures may not be recognized as epilepsy, and an observer may think that the child is daydreaming.

Partial seizures arise from a specific part of the brain. In the *Jacksonian type,* or focal type, the seizure begins with jerking of one part of the body and then spreads to other parts of the body. The person usually does not lose consciousness.

Some individuals experience strange sensations, such as tingling, smelling odors, and seeing images or hearing voices. When these sensations occur before a seizure, they are known as auras, a kind of warning of an impending attack.

Some types of seizures trigger bizarre behavior not under the person's control that is often not recognized as a seizure. There are many kinds of seizures, and some people have more than one kind.

To help a person who has a grand mal seizure, clear the area of hard objects, but do not try to restrict the person. Place a pillow, jacket, or other soft object under the head. Do not force anything into the mouth if the teeth are clenched. Turn the head to the side to provide an open airway. And when the seizure is over, provide reassurance to orient the person to time and place, and explain that he or she had a seizure since the person may not be aware of what happened. The rigid body, the twitching, and the loss of consciousness may cause observers to panic, but it is not necessary to call an ambulance unless the seizure lasts longer than ten minutes or the person is not breathing properly. Prolonged or repeated seizures (called *status epilepticus*) with respiratory problems are a life-threatening medical emergency.

Special tests used in diagnosing a seizure disorder include an EEG, or electroencephalogram, which records the electrical activity in the person's brain, and CAT scan and MRI, which are brain imaging techniques that can show abnormalities in brain structures.

In about half the cases of epilepsy, the cause is unknown. Among the known causes are the following: injuries to the brain during birth, infectious disease such as brain abscess or inflammation of the membranes of the brain or spinal cord, poisoning by toxins such as lead, mercury, and carbon monoxide, abnormalities in body chemistry, brain tumors, and stroke.

One of the most common causes of epilepsy is head injury from an accident. Wearing seat belts and safety harnesses while riding in automobiles, wearing helmets while bicycling, skateboarding, and in contact sports, and being aware of your limitations when climbing cliffs and mountains and before diving into water can help to protect against head injury that may result in epilepsy.

There are many drugs available to treat the various forms of epilepsy. About half the people treated for the disorder remain completely seizure-free indefinitely, and the frequency of seizures can be reduced in all but about 5 to 10 percent of cases. When the seizure disorder is caused by injury to a specific area in the brain, surgery can remove the damaged tissue that causes the electrical storms.

For most epileptics, staying seizure-free means taking medicine at the correct times, eating right, and getting enough rest and relaxation. It also means avoiding seizure triggers if at all possible. Such triggers may include flashing lights, breathing too quickly, loud noises, video games, and certain odors.

MULTIPLE SCLEROSIS (MS)

About 300,000 Americans have this progressive disease and probably developed it in their twenties or thirties. The disease may follow an irregular course, with periods when there are no symptoms. As MS gradually worsens, slurred speech, muscle spasms, vision loss, paralysis, and other problems may occur. However, the disease does not always result in severe disability.

The problems associated with MS can be traced to damaged areas of the nervous system. Nerve tracts in the human brain and spinal cord

Tiffany was in her second year at college when she had an attack of double vision and some weakness and tingling in one arm. These symptoms disappeared after a few days, but they returned several times during the year. By her senior year, Tiffany was having many severe episodes and her one leg was quite weak. She had some muscle spasms, dizziness, and she walked with a weaving gait. The symptoms went away and returned time and time again. A neurologist, testing with magnetic resonance imaging (MRI), found damage to some of her nerve pathways and diagnosed her disease as multiple sclerosis, or MS.

are sheathed in a covering called *myelin*. This sheath acts as an insulating material and makes it possible for speedy passage of electrical impulses along the nerves. It protects the fibers in the same way that insulation shields electrical wires. In MS, myelin becomes inflamed, swollen, and detached from the fibers. After a time it is replaced by patches of scar tissue that are left over the fiber. As a result, some of the nerve impulses are stopped or slowed at the damaged areas and do not reach their destination.

Although the cause of this damage to the nervous system is unknown, there may be genetic factors at the root of it. Some medical researchers believe that MS may result from a process in which a person's immune cells attack myelin. Scientists continue to search for causes, for better treatments, and for a cure. Drugs can reduce muscle spasms and shorten the episodes. Therapy to strengthen muscles, as well as various devices, help patients remain independent. Since the course of MS is unpredictable, counseling can be useful to many patients and their families.

The search for new drugs to stop the course of MS continues; some have been approved and are now in use.

PARKINSON'S DISEASE

Parkinson's is a progressive disease that affects about 1 in every 100 people over the age of sixty, striking men more often than women. It is primarily an affliction of older persons but about 5 percent of the cases occur under the age of sixty. One of the most common symptoms is trembling of the hands and other parts of the body, although several other things (including one disease that runs in families and is benign) cause trembling. In Parkinson's, the trembling is due to reduced levels of the chemical dopamine, which the brain is not producing in normal amounts.

Parkinson's causes some slowing and stiffening of muscular activity and a tendency for the limbs to be rigid. Patients with Parkinson's disease usually remain intellectually intact. Other symptoms that develop as time goes by may include difficulty in speaking and walking. A person with Parkinson's may walk either bent backward or falling forward and sometimes seems to freeze in one position.

In Parkinson's, there is degeneration of the part of the brain known as the *substantia nigra,* causing an abnormal chemical balance. The levels of dopamine are reduced and acetylcholine, another chemical, is overactive. Several drugs that increase dopamine levels can help patients, but in time, their effect may wear off. More aggressive treatment includes an operation in which small but carefully chosen parts of the brain are destroyed to stop the trembling. In one kind of operation that is still experimental, tissue from stillborn embryos is transplanted in the brain to replenish the damaged tissue of the adult patient. Surgery is not available or appropriate for everyone with Parkinson's disease. Although there is no cure, treatments help to control symptoms.

REYE'S SYNDROME

Reye's syndrome is a serious childhood disease that begins after another disease such as flu, chicken pox, or other viral illness. Aspirin may increase the risk of Reye's syndrome, and labels on bottles warn about this. The disease can be serious, even causing death in about 10 percent of the cases.

Courtney's father awoke one morning confused about who he was and where he was. Courtney called 911, and the ambulance took him to the emergency clinic where his condition was diagnosed as a TIA (transient ischemic attack), or small stroke. Although he had amnesia for a few hours, he was completely normal afterward.

To find out more about what had happened in his brain, the doctor ordered a test known as magnetic resonance imaging (MRI), which showed that part of his brain had been denied oxygen for a brief time. Here, some of the brain cells had died but others took over their function. This mild stroke was a warning that a more severe stroke might follow.

Courtney's father was told to watch for other warning signs of stroke such as weakness or numbness on one side, difficulty in speaking or understanding speech or complete loss of speech, loss of vision or blurred vision in one eye, and loss of balance. He followed the doctor's orders to lose weight, reduce his blood pressure with medication, and exercise more. These measures could help to prevent a stroke in many people.

Signs and symptoms vary, but after the initial viral infection, there is a brief recovery period. Then there are symptoms such as vomiting, drowsiness, agitation, and sometimes loss of consciousness and/or seizures. Early treatment may save a child's life. In the hospital, the disease is treated with intravenous fluids to help restore the chemical balance in the blood and reduce swelling in the brain.

STROKE

Strokes are the third leading cause of death in the United States (after heart disease and cancer), and many people still believe that little can be done to prevent the disabilities and death that they can cause. Today, a new treatment is helping many patients, but it must be given within three hours of having the stroke. A new drug called TPA may help tens of thousands of the 500,000 Americans who have strokes each year, but it is important for them to call for help at once.

What exactly is a stroke? It is a brain attack that occurs when a blood vessel bringing oxygen and nutrients to part of the brain becomes clogged or bursts. Being deprived of oxygen-rich blood causes injury or death to nerve cells, or neurons, in the brain. If the damage is severe, it may cause death of the person, but most people who have strokes survive.

While stroke is most common among the elderly, it is also the third leading cause of death among middle-aged people. The young can suffer from strokes, too, but strokes in the young are often tied to another disease, such as sickle cell anemia. (See chapter 15, "Disorders of the Blood.") There is a high risk of stroke among intravenous drug users. Cocaine use has also been linked to stroke, even in first-time users.

After a stroke, a person may have damage ranging from very little to severe. Difficulty in speaking, memory loss, and being unable to walk are just a few of the many problems that can result. Since different areas of the brain control different abilities and different parts of the body, the effects of a stroke depend on which part of the brain is injured and the amount of injury.

New medicines, such as blood thinners and clot busters, and other advances in prevention, treatment, and speech and physical therapy have brightened the outlook for stroke survivors and those at risk.

Overcoming damage from a stroke depends on the extent of the brain injury, the attitude of the patient, the skill of the rehabilitation team, and the cooperation of friends and family.

9

Mental Illness

During their lifetime, one of every five adults in the United States will suffer from a mental illness that is severe enough to require treatment. Millions of others will have problems that are less serious yet prevent them from enjoying life. Some do not seek help because they do not know treatment is available or they are afraid of being labeled "crazy." In 1840, there was only one official category of mental illness, called idiocy/insanity. Now several hundred disorders are listed and defined in an official reference manual called the *Diagnostic and Statistical Manual of Mental Disorders* (DSM). Although there is no exact dividing line between "normal" and "abnormal," a mental disorder can be defined as a psychological condition or pattern of behavior that causes distress or problems that interfere with a person's ability to function. Mental illness may strike anyone, at any age, but some disorders commonly begin in childhood.

ATTENTION DEFICIT/ HYPERACTIVITY DISORDER (ADHD)

By 1996, attention deficit/hyperactivity disorder (ADHD) had become the most common childhood psychiatric disorder diagnosed in the United States. Although the behavior associated with ADHD (see sidebar) used to be blamed on deliberate badness or wrong parenting, researchers now believe that these children are born with some impairment in their brains. No one knows exactly what the problem is, and it cannot be diagnosed by a blood test or X rays. About four times more boys than girls are affected. Symptoms vary, and it is often difficult to distinguish ADHD from other disorders that cause similar symptoms, such as learning disabilities, depression, or anxiety, or from normal children's behavior.

Fortunately, a medication called Ritalin can help children with ADHD; it changes the brain chemistry and results in remarkable improvement. One boy called it his organizing medicine. But pills alone are not a magic cure; behavior modification or other kinds of help are necessary. The use of Ritalin soared after 1990, and many

Charley was a bright, alert, active baby who grew even more active as a toddler. By age three, he had became a whirlwind, running from one room to another, tearing up his picture books instead of looking at them, pulling clothes from the dresser drawers, hammering his toys to pieces, unable to sit still without fidgeting, and acting as though driven by a motor. When he began school, his overly active behavior became more troublesome because it was disruptive for the rest of the class. Charley could not remain in his seat and kept getting up and walking around. It often seemed that he was not listening to the teacher, and he rarely finished assigned tasks. His work was sloppy, and he made careless mistakes. He was easily distracted, and he sometimes forgot what he was supposed to do. He talked too much, interrupting others and blurting out answers before the teacher could finish her questions. He was impulsive, acting before thinking, and he often became involved in fights with other children. He drove his teacher to distraction. Was Charley bad, stupid, or crazy? Not at all. He had a condition known as attention deficit/hyperactivity disorder.

psychiatrists think it is prescribed far too often to children who may not need it. Equally worrisome is the fact that a black market has sprung up, and "Vitamin R" is sold in schools and playgrounds as a cheap way to get high.

AUTISTIC DISORDER (AUTISM)

> A week after he was born, Rafael's mother noticed that he was not a cuddly baby. He did not respond to his mother's voice or touch with coos or smiles, even after several months, and he seemed more interested in watching the mobile hanging over his crib than in the people around him. At first, his mother thought he was deaf, but after several consultations and examinations by a specialist during the next year, she was told that Rafael had probably been born with a type of rare disorder of development known as autism.

Autistic disorder is another condition that shows itself early in life. Although in the past, the disorder was blamed on mothers who were cold and indifferent to their babies, experts now know that these children begin life with their brains "wired wrong."

Every autistic child is different, but all suffer from very abnormal development of communication skills and an inability to interact normally with other people. Some children never learn to speak, while others have their own language or repeat certain words or phrases over and over. Some repeat the same movements endlessly. They seem emotionally detached from others and are more interested in objects than in people. They may have behavior problems such as hyperactivity, aggressiveness, and temper tantrums, often becoming upset if a rigid daily routine is not followed. About 75 percent of autistic children function at a retarded level, but a small number are able to live on their own and work.

Asperger's disorder is a related condition, in which there is no delay in development of language or other skills, but there is a severe disturbance in the ability to interact socially and to understand others' feelings. Despite her problems, one remarkable woman with this disorder was able to obtain a graduate degree, carry out research at a university, and even write a book.

DEPRESSION

Eighteen million people in the United States suffer from depression, but only one in three gets help, even though treatment is available. Most people do not get help because the problem is not recognized, or because they think they should be able to snap out of it on their own. But serious depression is not like the temporary sad mood or blues that everyone occasionally experiences. A severe depression may last for months or years and is very painful and disabling. Fifteen percent of people hospitalized for depression eventually commit suicide.

People who suffer from serious depression typically have symptoms that include persistent sad or empty mood, loss of interest in ordinary activities, decreased energy, fatigue, insomnia or sleeping too much, loss of appetite or overeating, difficulty with concentration and memory, thoughts of death or

Fifteen-year-old Kwame was a good student who had many friends and enjoyed sports and music. When he returned to school after winter vacation, he began having trouble paying attention to his schoolwork, and his grades dropped. He stopped playing the drums at weekly music sessions with his friends. He appeared to have lost interest in everything, and he seemed preoccupied and withdrawn. Then he gave his drums and guitar to his best friend, explaining that he would not need them any longer, and he asked his friend to keep this information to himself. But his friend knew that this kind of information should not be kept secret, because Kwame's behavior was a clue that he was thinking about suicide. Kwame was fortunate; he got help, and his depression lifted quickly.

suicide, and feelings of hopelessness, helplessness, worth-lessness, and guilt.

Sometimes people do not recognize depression in chil-dren and adolescents because they may not appear sad, but instead may act aggressive, irritable, angry, or obnoxious. Young children often cannot express sad feelings in words, so they express them by actions. Sudden onset of "bad" be-havior in children is a warning sign that something is wrong.

There are several kinds of depression. Many people expe-rience recurrent episodes of depression during their lives. Some have repeated mood swings that cycle between inap-propriate highs (mania) and lows (depression). This is called *manic-depressive disorder* or *bipolar disorder*. The manic stage is characterized by an excessively elated mood, increased energy, racing thoughts, nonstop talking, grandi-ose ideas, feelings of being invincible, and impaired judg-ment.

Depressive disorders are biological. They run in families and are marked by disturbances of certain chemical sub-stances in the brain. It is important to seek medical advice for depression that lasts for more than a couple of weeks, because almost everyone with a mood disorder can be treated successfully with medication that corrects the chemical imbalance.

EATING DISORDERS

Eating disorders are severe disturbances in eating behavior and are among the most serious illnesses that affect teenag-ers and young adults. Although some males are affected, 90 percent are females. It is estimated that about 1 percent of the young women in the United States have an eating disorder. All have an overwhelming fear of gaining weight.

Some accomplish this by refusing food, adhering to strict diets, or exercising intensely. No matter how thin they are, they think they are too fat. The malnutrition resulting from not eating properly may cause serious damage to lungs, heart, and other organs, menstrual problems, and it may even lead to death. This eating disorder is known as *anorexia nervosa.*

Another common eating disorder is the binge-and-purge disorder known as *bulimia nervosa.* People with this disorder go on eating binges, after which they force themselves to vomit or take laxatives to eliminate the food. Vomiting and purging may cause serious abnormalities in body fluids and chemicals. Moreover, frequent vomiting may cause damage to teeth as stomach acid eats away at the enamel. A number of people have a mixed disorder; they have anorexia and also go on occasional binges. People with eating disorders feel that food controls their lives. They are obsessed with thoughts about food and eating, and they cannot stop their compulsive behavior.

Christy Henrich was a nationally ranked gymnast who weighed less than sixty pounds when she died at the age of twenty-two, a victim of the fear of being fat. She suffered from an eating disorder and literally starved herself to death.

There is no single cause for eating disorders, but experts note that there are many risk factors. Many people with anorexia and bulimia have a great need to control their lives, low self-esteem, and a drive to be perfect. Some studies have suggested that there is an inherited tendency for developing an eating disorder. Culture also plays a role. In much of our society, thinness is considered desirable. Researchers at the University of Arizona found that 90 percent

Sally was typical of those who suffer from the common eating disorder known as bulimia nervosa. She appeared normal, she was not underweight, and she kept her eating problem so well hidden that not even her boyfriend knew about it. Although Sally ate regular meals, several times a week she indulged in binges, eating huge amounts of food. Feeling depressed and tense one evening, she began with a meal in her favorite Chinese restaurant. On her way home, she gobbled down four hot dogs that she bought from a street vendor. Then she picked up some ice cream and a bag of cookies at the supermarket, and at home she ate all the cookies and a quart of chocolate ice cream. After stuffing herself with food, she went to the bathroom and forced herself to vomit. Sometimes she took laxatives to get rid of the food she ate. By vomiting and purging, she was able to keep her weight normal. She felt ashamed and guilty and totally out of control, but she was not able to stop herself from bingeing.

of the white junior high and high school girls interviewed were dissatisfied with their weight. In contrast, they found that 70 percent of the African-American girls they studied were satisfied with their bodies, and most said that it was better to be a bit overweight than underweight. African-American girls believe that attributes such as the "right attitude" and "how you carry yourself" are more important than size. For many black teens, a full figure signifies health and fertility. It is not surprising that eating disorders are relatively uncommon among African-American teenagers.

If you think you have any of the signs of an eating disorder, severely restricting your food intake, exercising excessively to control your weight, or bingeing and then vomiting or purging, you should seek professional help. There are many organizations that can assist you. To get in touch with the American Anorexia/Bulimia Association, see the "For Further Information" section at the end of this book.

OBSESSIVE-COMPULSIVE DISORDER (OCD)

Considered very rare in the past, OCD is now known to affect about 2 percent of the population, commonly striking in young adulthood or even earlier.

No one knows exactly what causes it; one expert calls OCD a "hiccup in the brain."

People with OCD are tormented with obsessions—unwanted ideas and thoughts that occur repeatedly and cause anxiety. To control the anxiety, they develop compulsions, or meaningless rituals they feel compelled to carry out over and over again. Typical compulsions are excessive handwashing, house-cleaning, and scrubbing, counting or touching objects, and checking locks on doors repeatedly. One woman felt compelled to scrub everything that was brought into her house, and she made her children shower before entering their rooms, for fear of contamination with germs. Some people must perform so many rituals that they have no time for anything else in their lives. Although people with OCD suffer much embarrassment, anxiety, and often depression, they can be helped with medication and psychological therapy.

> Josh appeared to be a normal thirteen-year-old who was a good student and popular with his classmates. But after the family moved to another city, he suddenly began showing some strange behavior. He had to perform two hours of exercises before going to bed each night; he checked every door before entering a room; he repeated phrases over and over again; and he was unable to eat a bowl of cereal unless he placed the spoon exactly the "right" way. He felt compelled to do these things, even though he realized that they made no sense. Josh had a very disturbing condition called obsessive-compulsive disorder, or OCD.

PANIC DISORDER

People with panic disorder experience *panic attacks*, episodes of intense fear accompanied by physical symptoms (see sidebar). Researchers believe that they occur when the brain's normal way of reacting to a threat is aroused inappropriately, and they have found evidence linking panic disorder with increased activity in certain parts of the brain and with abnormalities in brain chemistry. Panic disorder

Rekha was finishing her first year of college, and she was studying hard for her final exams. As she walked back to her room from the library one evening, her heart suddenly began to pound, she felt light-headed and dizzy, and she was seized by the thought that something awful was about to happen or that she might die. She was afraid she might lose control of herself and go crazy. The episode lasted only a few minutes, but it was so scary that she made an appointment to see her doctor. She did not have heart disease, and she was not going crazy. She had experienced a panic attack.

usually begins in young adulthood, and women are affected twice as often as men. About 3 million people in the United States will experience panic disorder at some time.

Some people with panic disorder may feel anxious all the time because they worry about having another attack. This may lead to the development of irrational fears called *phobias* about situations or places where an attack has occurred. About one-third of all people with panic disorder develop a fear of leaving their home or neighborhood; this is called *agoraphobia*, and it is very disabling. It prevents the person from going to work or shopping and makes him or her dependent on family and friends.

Fortunately, there is effective treatment for panic disorder and phobias. Medications to reduce anxiety and psychotherapy to help the person change thought patterns and behavior can benefit most people.

It is normal to experience anxiety occasionally, but severe or prolonged anxiety is not normal. Many mental disorders cause anxiety; panic disorder and phobias are only two examples. Certain drugs and some physical conditions may also cause anxiety, so it is important to have a medical checkup in order to rule out other problems.

SCHIZOPHRENIA

Schizophrenia is a serious chronic mental illness that affects between 1 and 2 percent of the population of the

United States, usually striking in adolescence or early adulthood; only in rare cases does it begin in children under the age of twelve. It is a biological disorder in which there is a defect in the way the brain sorts out and interprets information, with the result that thinking is disordered and illogical. Thoughts and ideas may be disconnected and jumbled. In some people with schizophrenia, the disorganization is so severe that their speech makes no sense to others. Some have delusional ideas based on faulty perceptions of reality. A *delusion* is a false, often bizarre belief that the individual is firmly convinced is true. It often involves the idea that the individual is being persecuted or harmed in some way.

One delusional young man refused to watch a certain game show on television because he believed that the host was controlling his thoughts. One day, state troopers discovered him on the highway driving 100 miles an hour with his eyes closed. He believed he had magical powers that kept him from harm and that he would be resurrected immediately if he died. No one was able to convince him that these beliefs were false and irrational.

Some people with schizophrenia hear voices; they are experiencing *hallucinations,* or false perceptions of sense. Hallucinations may also involve false sensations of bodily feelings, smell, taste, or vision. People with schizophrenia often show inappropriate emotional reactions and may have difficulty relating to other people.

Although there is no cure, treatment for schizophrenia is available. Antipsychotic drugs, which block certain brain chemicals, act to reduce delusions and hallucinations, lessen confusion of thinking, and relieve anxiety. About 25 percent of people with schizophrenia recover completely, 50 percent show various degrees of improvement, and 25 percent do not improve. Some people with schizophrenia need to be hospitalized for a period of time until their thinking and judgment improve. Many need long-term psychotherapy and support in addition to medication.

Schizophrenia is an illness surrounded by myths, ignorance, and fear. It is a brain disease, and the tendency to develop it is inherited. It is not caused by bad parents. Because this disease affects thinking, speech, and behavior, many individuals with schizophrenia speak and act oddly, and may even appear scary to others. But most are not dangerous; they are more likely to be confused and fearful.

It is often difficult to know when professional help is needed for mental problems such as schizophrenia and depression, but there are some important warning signs. A marked change in behavior may be a sign of trouble. Sometimes, a stressful event like a death in the family or loss of a job can trigger a severe emotional reaction. Another warning sign is extreme anxiety or nervousness that is not related to a normal concern such as passing an exam or paying the rent. If a person becomes abusive, rude, or unreasonably suspicious of others, or behaves violently, help is needed. In a crisis, if a person becomes dangerous to himself/herself or others, you should call the police. There are many services available to help people with mental problems, and they are listed in the telephone book under various headings such as "Emergency or Crisis Services," "Hospitals," and "Mental Health Clinics."

Hormonal Disorders

Hormones are complex chemical substances that regulate many functions of the body. They are produced by endocrine glands, such as the thyroid, adrenals, sex glands, and pituitary, and secreted directly into the bloodstream. Hormones act as chemical signals to cells to change their behavior in a specific way. Many of their effects are very dramatic, such as shaping embryos into male or female, and controlling physical growth, metabolism, sleep, and numerous other functions. When there is too much or too little of a hormone, serious diseases can result.

ACROMEGALY AND GIGANTISM

These disorders are caused by *hyperpituitarism*, a condition in which too much growth hormone is secreted by the pituitary gland, a small gland hanging from the underside of the brain.

When an excess of growth hormone occurs in children or adolescents, the condition is known as gigantism. It is a

When Ashley was eight years old, she was taller than her twelve-year-old sister. At the rate she was growing, she would soon be taller than her father. When her doctor suggested that she had a disease known as gigantism, Ashley thought he was joking. The tallest known person with gigantism reached a height of almost nine feet, so she and her family were eager for treatment that would slow her fast rate of growth. Tests showed that she had an oversupply of growth hormone caused by a small tumor on her pituitary gland. Surgery to remove the tumor or radiation to destroy it would cure Ashley's problem.

rare condition caused by a tumor of the pituitary gland. Most tall children do not have a hormonal disorder; they are just programmed by their genes to be tall, but when growth is far above normal standards, gigantism may be responsible. A doctor should be consulted if there is a question about excessive growth.

When the pituitary secretes excessive growth hormone in adults, the condition is known as acromegaly. It is characterized by excessively large hands, feet, and jaw.

Pituitary excessive growth abnormalities can be treated by surgical removal of a tumor, radiation therapy, or by drugs to control the release of the hormone.

DIABETES MELLITUS

Diabetes mellitus (*mellitus* means "honey-sweet") is one of the most common chronic diseases in the United States. It occurs if special cells in the pancreas do not produce enough of the hormone insulin, or if the body cannot use this insulin effectively. Insulin regulates the body's use of glucose (sugar); it is needed to transport glucose into the cells, where the glucose is used for energy or stored. When there is not enough insulin, very high levels of glucose accumulate in the blood and spill into the urine.

There are two forms of diabetes: insulin-dependent (also called Type I or juvenile onset) and noninsulin-dependent (Type II or adult onset). Most of the people with Type II diabetes develop it when they are over forty years old, and most are overweight. In both cases, the symptoms are the same (see sidebar).

Symptoms usually develop more rapidly in juvenile diabetes. Sometimes there are no obvious symptoms in people with adult onset diabetes, and the disease is discovered when a routine test shows sugar in the urine.

The "sugar disease," as it is sometimes called, cannot be cured, but it can be controlled by insulin injections and careful attention to diet

Common symptoms of diabetes are:

- Excessive thirst
- Frequent urination
- Weight loss
- Fatigue or weakness
- Frequent infections

so that the amount of glucose in the blood remains at a normal level. People with juvenile diabetes need insulin shots because their bodies no not produce insulin. (Before these shots were available, this type of diabetes was always fatal.) But some people with adult onset diabetes can control their disease without insulin shots by keeping to a strict diet, exercising, and losing weight. Some may also need to take drugs by mouth that lower their blood sugar.

Imagine the problem of a teen who must avoid junk food, eat regular meals with carefully calculated amounts of various nutrients, monitor her blood glucose regularly, and inject herself with insulin every day. Some children deal with this easily, but when they become teenagers, it is often much more difficult.

Strenuous exercise, illness, surgery, and even stress caused by emotional problems can change the amount of insulin required to maintain a normal glucose level.

Diabetes control has been called a balancing act. Most young diabetics know that if they do not manage their diabetes properly, the results can be severe. If the blood sugar level falls too low, a condition known as *hypoglycemia* or insulin shock occurs. It can be caused by conditions such as too much insulin or prolonged exercise. The symptoms include shaking, sweating, lightheadedness, anxiety, loss of coordination, and sometimes confusion. If these symptoms are not treated immediately by consuming food or drink high in sugar in order to increase the blood sugar, unconsciousness may result. If the person is unconscious, glucose must be given by vein. Hypoglycemia can be life threatening and needs to be treated immediately. Sometimes it is mistaken for drunkenness, and death occurs because proper treatment is not given.

Complications of diabetes that develop over a period of years include eye, kidney, and heart disease, but new treatments are reducing the number of cases of blindness due to diabetes. Diabetes can reduce the flow of blood to the legs and feet and dull the ability to feel heat, cold, and pain. Skin and foot care are important, because diabetics have a higher risk of infection than other people.

Despite the many challenges they face in keeping their disease in check, and despite the risk of complications, most people with diabetes are able to lead normal lives.

DWARFISM

Too little growth hormone (*hypopituitarism*) in childhood can cause slow growth or late puberty and can cause dwarfism. Sometimes dwarfism can be diagnosed in the first few months of life, but symptoms often develop slowly. Untreated, these children typically grow to a height of about four feet, but their proportions are normal. Dwarfism may be caused by conditions such as a tumor on the front portion of the pituitary or an absent or undeveloped gland at birth.

In addition to growth hormone, the anterior, or front, part of the pituitary gland manufactures other important hormones that regulate the sex glands, thyroid, and adrenals. If there is a deficiency of all these hormones (called *panhypopituitarism*), these glands do not function properly, and the consequences may be life threatening. Adults as well as children may have a deficiency of pituitary hormones.

Tests of this condition include measurement of pituitary hormones in the blood, tests of other glands, and CAT (computerized axial tomography) scan, MRI (magnetic resonance imaging), or X rays to check for a tumor of the pituitary.

Treatment involves giving growth hormone before puberty. A child may grow as much as four to six inches in the first year of treatment. Treatment with other hormones, such as adrenal or thyroid hormones, may also be needed.

HYPERTHYROIDISM

Hyperthyroidism (Graves' disease) results from an overproduction of thyroid hormone. Symptoms are an enlarged thyroid gland, nervousness, tremor, palpitations, weight loss, sweating, and heat intolerance. In some cases, the eyeballs protrude abnormally. The presence of the disease can be confirmed by laboratory tests that show high levels of thyroid hormones. Treatment to decrease the amount of thyroid hormone consists of giving antithyroid drugs or radioactive iodine, or performing surgery to remove part of the thyroid.

HYPOTHYROIDISM

When the level of thyroid hormone in the blood is below normal in adults, early symptoms include sensitivity to cold, forgetfulness, fatigue, constipation, and unexplained weight gain. Other symptoms include dry, flaky skin; puffy face, hands, and feet; and hair loss. A sensitive laboratory test can determine the level of thyroid hormone in the body, and giving thyroid hormone can raise the level to normal.

In babies, a condition sometimes called *infantile cretinism* is due to a deficiency of thyroid hormone beginning during fetal development or early in infancy. On rare occasions, the good baby may be suffering from this condition. Such a baby is generally inactive, sleeps excessively, and rarely cries. When he or she does cry, the sound is unusually hoarse. Other signs include a large, protruding tongue, respiratory difficulties, cold skin, slow pulse, and jaundice. If these babies are not treated early, they suffer irreversible mental retardation, stunted growth, and bone and muscle atrophy. Thyroid hormone replacement treatment must continue throughout life.

Disorders of the Reproductive System

The reproductive system, like the other systems of the body, is subject to such disorders as inborn defects, hormonal disorders, cancer, and infections. Some infections are discussed in chapter 16; the following are a few examples of other conditions.

DYSMENORRHEA (PAINFUL MENSTRUATION)

Many young women experience painful menstruation; it is the most common problem related to the female reproductive system and a major cause of absenteeism from school and work. Dysmenorrhea may be the result of conditions such as infection, fibroid tumors of the uterus, or other disorders. In most cases, no cause can be identified, although hormonal imbalance may play a part, and psychological factors may have an influence. However, this does not

Male Reproductive System

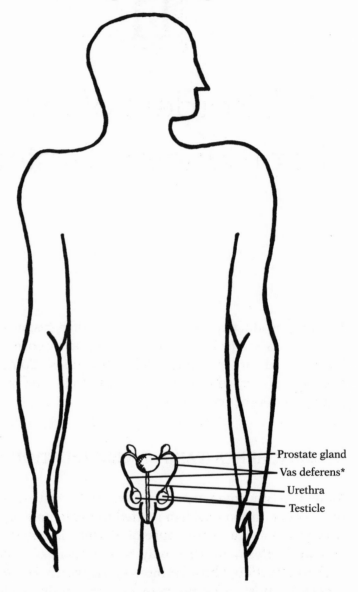

Prostate gland
Vas deferens*
Urethra
Testicle

Vas deferens: Tube that carries sperm from each testicle through the prostate gland, and into the back of the urethra, below where it meets the bladder; the bladder (not shown in the illustration) lies just above the prostate gland.

Female Reproductive System

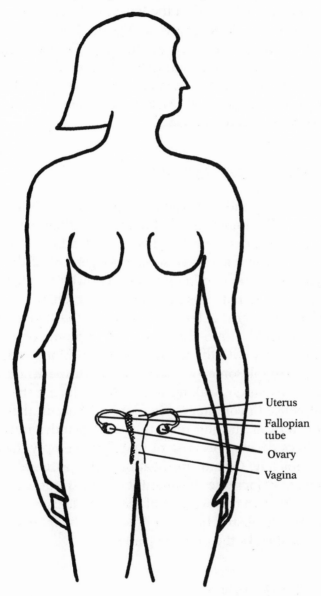

Uterus

Fallopian
tube

Ovary

Vagina

mean that the pain is all in your head. The pain is sharp and cramping and is located in the lower abdomen, sometimes extending to the back, thighs, and groin. It is often accompanied by symptoms such as bloating, diarrhea, painful breasts, headache, and irritability. It generally starts just before or at the onset of menstruation. Dysmenorrhea can be helped by aspirin, NSAIDs (nonsteroidal anti-inflammatory drugs), and exercise.

ENLARGED PROSTATE GLAND

The prostate gland is a walnut-sized structure found only in males; it lies under the bladder, surrounding the urethra in the area where the urethra leaves the bladder. Most men over fifty years of age have some enlargement of the prostate gland, but no one knows precisely why this happens. Enlargement is not prostate cancer. (See chapter 14.) As the gland enlarges, it tends to obstruct the flow of urine from the bladder into the urethra. Symptoms of this enlargement vary with the amount of obstruction; some men have no troublesome problems. Others experience more frequent urination, waking many times during the night; incontinence (involuntary urination) may occur; there may be difficulty in starting urination; and bladder infections sometimes develop because of inability to empty the bladder completely. Certain medications such as nasal decongestants may increase the amount of constriction. In some cases, surgery to remove part of the prostate is necessary to relieve severe obstruction, but others can be treated with a drug that shrinks the prostate gland.

HYPOGONADISM

Hypogonadism is a condition resulting from decreased production of male hormone. It is sometimes due to damage to certain cells in the testes that secrete testosterone and to other cells that produce sperm. In other cases, it is caused by abnormalities of the pituitary gland, which interacts with the sex glands. The symptoms of hypogonadism may include delayed puberty, small genital organs, low sperm count, underdeveloped muscles, sparse or absent body and facial hair, and high-pitched voice. Depending on the underlying cause, treatment consists of hormone replacement.

Boys with this disorder often feel very worried about their slow development and lack of masculine appearance, and they may have a poor self-image. Other boys may tease them, and they may be reluctant to join in activities for this reason. Parents and friends need to be understanding and supportive.

PREMENSTRUAL SYNDROME (PMS)

PMS is a group of symptoms that begin about a week or more before the onset of menstruation each month. It is a real disorder that is estimated to affect more than 70 percent of all women at some time. No one is certain of the cause, but it may be related to hormonal changes. The symptoms may vary greatly from one person to another and range from mild to severe. They include skin problems such as acne or rash; abdominal cramps or bloating; muscle aches, backache, or joint pain; heart palpitations; dizziness, headache, clumsiness, tingling or numbness in hands; psychological symptoms such as depression, anxiety, mood swings, anger, absentmindedness, and accident-prone behavior; and food cravings.

Treatment of PMS consists of relieving the symptoms and avoiding triggers. Aspirin and other pain relievers, medication to reduce excess fluid in the body, vitamins, avoidance of caffeine, and a low-salt diet have all been found to reduce symptoms. In addition, reducing stress, exercising, eating nutritious foods, and getting enough sleep are all important. Joining a support group can also be helpful.

UNDESCENDED TESTES

The testes develop in the abdomen during gestation, and they normally descend into the scrotum about a month before birth. However, it is not uncommon for a baby to be born with one testis or both testes still undescended. Sometimes hormones are given to correct the condition. If the testes do not descend by the age of one year, surgery is usually recommended, because leaving them in the abdomen can result in sterility, and also may increase the chance of testicular cancer.

12

Disorders of the Skin

The envelope of skin that covers the body acts as protection against microbes and harmful substances, blocks the loss of body fluids, and helps regulate temperature. Any kind of skin eruption is commonly referred to as a rash; there are many, and their causes vary. Some are indications of internal disease—viral illnesses such as chicken pox and some cancers, for example. Skin problems are very common; at least 30 percent of Americans have skin disorders requiring a physician's care.

ACNE

Almost every part of the body is covered with hair, visible or invisible. Each hair grows from a tiny pit known as a follicle, and there is an oil-producing gland in each one. In adolescents, these oil-secreting glands tend to produce excessive amounts of the secretion, known as sebum, and plugs form in skin pores. This may result in whiteheads or, when the sebum darkens, blackheads. Bacteria may invade

91

the sebum and cause inflammation, pus, and swelling—that is, acne pimples. Squeezing or picking pimples can cause tender red lumps with white, pus-filled centers.

Acne, although it can be distressing, is considered a normal part of growing up. In mild cases, nonprescription creams and lotions are effective, but scrubbing the skin may make the problem worse. Dermatologists can usually help in severe cases.

ATHLETE'S FOOT

Athlete's foot is caused by a fungus that grows on the skin, mainly between and under the toes. Hot, humid weather and tight shoes and socks encourage the growth of the fungus. It is often spread at swimming pools and gymnasiums. If you have athlete's foot, dry your feet thoroughly after bathing or swimming, and apply an antifungal spray, powder, or cream to the affected area. Open sandals, shoes with porous innersoles and uppers, and socks made from natural fibers are recommended. If these measures do not help, consult a doctor.

ATOPIC DERMATITIS (INFANTILE ECZEMA)

Atopic dermatitis is one of a group of skin rashes known as the *eczemas*, or *eczematous dermatitis*. They are marked by the presence of bumps, small blisters that burst, itching, and red patches. Atopic dermatitis is a common type of eczema that occurs in babies, and is often associated with allergies. Although it sometimes occurs in adults, atopic dermatitis usually comes and goes, and then disappears at adolescence.

CONTACT DERMATITIS

Contact dermatitis is a skin inflammation caused by direct physical contact with an irritant such as acid or strong detergent, or with a substance that causes an allergic reaction. Paints, dyes, glue, metal jewelry, hairspray, bubble bath, cosmetics, wool, and plants (especially poison oak, poison sumac, and poison ivy) are only a few of the substances that can cause contact dermatitis. Avoiding contact with the offending substance is the first step for treating the problem, but identifying the offender is sometimes difficult. Cortisone creams and ointments are effective treatment in most cases.

IMPETIGO

Impetigo is a very contagious bacterial skin infection that usually occurs around the mouth and nose, appearing as small blisters, which ooze and form yellowish brown crusts. It is more common in children than in adults. Impetigo is easily spread to other family members by the sharing of towels. Babies may suffer from impetigo all over their bodies, and this makes them very ill. A physician should be consulted in any case, so that antibiotic treatment can be prescribed to prevent the infection from spreading.

LICE

These tiny, but visible, insects suck blood from the skin of people of any age. Crab lice usually appear in hair around sex organs, but they may infest eyebrows, eyelashes, and other body hair. Children often spread head lice at school. They become aware of the lice because their bites cause itching in the affected areas. Lice eggs, called nits, look like tiny white grains clinging to the hair.

Medications are available to kill the lice. Combs, brushes, clothing, and bedsheets must be washed in hot water and, if possible, dried in a hot dryer.

PSORIASIS

Psoriasis is a common skin disease of unknown origin that causes the formation of red patches with silvery, scaly surfaces. In children, it commonly appears as small scaly dots. Psoriasis has an unpredictable course, flaring up and then subsiding. Stress, cuts, burns, and insect bites may trigger a flare-up. Exposure to sun may help, and several kinds of medications are available to control psoriasis and reduce the symptoms, but there is no cure. Keeping good general health habits is considered part of the treatment.

SKIN CANCER (SEE CHAPTER 14)

WARTS

Many myths are associated with warts; some people think they are caused by handling frogs or toads. The fact is that these small, bumpy growths on the skin are caused by a type of virus. They occur most often in children, generally on the hands, elbows, and knees, and they are painless and harmless. They are known as *plantar warts* when they occur on the soles of the feet. Many doctors think that the best treatment is no treatment, for warts tend to disappear spontaneously. Even if they are removed by chemicals or surgery, they often recur.

13

Disorders of Bones, Muscles, and Joints

Your body has 206 bones, many joints and ligaments, 600 different muscles, and tendons that attach muscles to bones. These structures support the body, and they are very vulnerable to injuries such as fractures and sprains. They may also be affected by conditions such as inherited diseases, disorders of metabolism, infection, and cancer.

GOUT

This condition, which affects the joints, is caused by overproduction of a substance called uric acid, due in some cases to an inherited defect in metabolism, and in others to various medical disorders. Uric acid salts are retained in the body and are deposited in the joints, causing pain and swelling. In the later stages of the disease, deposits of uric acid salts may form in other tissues.

Gout cannot be cured, but it can controlled by medications: some to reduce the amount of uric acid in the blood, and others to reduce inflammation. Avoiding alcohol and certain foods such as liver and seafood that raise the uric acid level, is also helpful, but severe limitation is not always necessary when uric acid–lowering drugs are taken.

MUSCULAR DYSTROPHY

The term *muscular dystrophy* refers to a rare group of inherited disorders marked by a progressive, painless wasting of muscles with no loss of feeling. The most common is the *Duchenne type*, which causes about half of the cases, and it affects only boys. It begins early in childhood, between the ages of three and five. As the muscles become damaged, they enlarge because they are replaced by fat and other tissue. A child with this disease walks with a waddling gait, falls easily, has trouble getting up, and has difficulty climbing stairs or raising his arms above his head. Most children with Duchenne-type dystrophy are confined to a wheelchair before they reach adolescence.

There are other types of muscular dystrophy that do not shorten the person's life, but Duchenne dystrophy usually causes death from heart failure, respiratory failure, or infection by age twenty. Unfortunately, no cure has been discovered. The Duchenne type is both sex-linked and recessive. If there is a history of this disease in a woman's family, there is a chance that she may be a carrier of the defective gene. If tests show that she is a carrier, and if she has a boy, there is a 50 percent chance that he will inherit the disease. Men, too, may carry the gene, and the actual disorder is confined to males.

Peter wondered why his grandmother's fingers were so bumpy and stiff that it was hard for her to button her dress. She always groaned when she rose from her chair, and when the weather was cold she complained that her "rheumatism" was worse. Peter's grandmother has one of the most common joint problems—a degenerative disorder called osteoarthritis. She called it rheumatism, but there is no such medical term.

OSTEOARTHRITIS

Almost everyone over age forty shows some signs of osteoarthritis on X rays, even if there are no symptoms. It is a consequence of aging, and not the same as rheumatoid arthritis. The smooth lining of the joint begins to deteriorate and become roughened or cracked, and the bone underneath becomes thickened. It affects mainly the larger joints such as hips and knees, but it can attack any joint in the body. Pain, stiffness, and swelling come and go over a period of years. If a joint is very painful, the person has a tendency not to use the affected joint; not using the muscles causes them to become wasted and weak.

No one knows exactly what causes osteoarthritis, but it is made worse by wear and tear. For this reason, even younger people may get it. Ballet dancers develop it in their feet from standing on their toes. It also affects football players and others who are exposed to repeated injuries. This kind of arthritis is not as bad as rheumatoid arthritis (discussed later in this chapter), and most people are not seriously hampered by it. Taking aspirin and other medications can relieve the pain and swelling. Exercise can help keep people with arthritis flexible and strong. Individuals who are overweight can benefit by losing weight to lessen the strain on their joints. Many older people with severe pain and disability have had successful surgery to replace their worn-out joints. Hip and knee replacements have allowed them to return to an active life, even participating in sports such as skiing.

OSTEOPOROSIS

Your bones are living structures, with old bone constantly being broken down and replaced with new bone. In osteoporosis, this balance is disturbed, and bone breaks down faster than it can be replaced. Calcium and other minerals are lost, and the bones become porous and brittle. Some causes of osteoporosis are kidney failure, certain hormone disorders, calcium-deficient diet, prolonged period of immobility, excessive alcohol consumption, and smoking. Small-boned women over the age of fifty have the greatest risk of getting osteoporosis, especially those who reach menopause at an early age.

Many people do not realize that they are losing bone mass, because the changes are slow and subtle and they have no symptoms.

Osteoporosis cannot be cured once the damage is done, but the rate of bone loss can be slowed. Research has shown that regular

Fifty-five-year-old Mara smoked heavily, didn't eat enough dairy products or other foods containing calcium, and was a couch potato. She noticed that she seemed to be getting shorter and more round-shouldered and that her back was becoming curved. Her doctor took X rays that showed some degeneration of the vertebrae, the small bones that make up the spine. Osteoporosis in these bones caused the changes in her appearance. People like Mara with weakened bones are at high risk for fractures.

exercise, especially weight-bearing exercise like walking or running, can keep your bones strong. Eating a diet rich in calcium is very important for both the young and old, in order to build strong bones and teeth. A woman who is approaching menopause should consult her physician about taking estrogen, since it is known that estrogen protects against osteoporosis. This hormone replacement therapy is not a suitable treatment for all women, but an alternative is available. A bone-strengthening drug approved by the FDA in 1995 has been shown to reduce the risk of fractures in elderly women with osteoporosis.

RHEUMATOID ARTHRITIS

Juvenile rheumatoid arthritis (sometimes called juvenile chronic arthritis or JCA) affects about 200,000 children in the United States. The exact cause is not known, but it may be due to an abnormality in which the immune system attacks joints and other tissues as if they were foreign bodies. One type of JCA is called *Still's disease.* (See sidebar.) A different form of JCA sometimes causes eye inflammation that can lead to blindness if not treated.

There is a good chance that children with JCA will recover with little or no disability. JCA is treated with aspirin, but sometimes NSAIDs (nonsteroidal anti-in-

Meryl's grandmother had suffered from arthritis for a long time so Meryl was familiar with the fact that arthritis can be very painful and sometimes very crippling. However, Meryl did not know that some kinds of arthritis can attack children. She learned this after going through a period when she felt tired, sore, and stiff. At first, Meryl's parents and her doctor thought she had the flu because she had attacks of high fever, rash, enlarged lymph nodes, and pains in her abdomen, in addition to stiffness. After doing some tests, her doctor diagnosed the problem as juvenile rheumatoid arthritis of the type know as Still's disease.

flammatory drugs) or other, more powerful drugs must be used. Physical therapy and exercise help prevent permanent stiffness and deformities.

The adult form of rheumatoid arthritis, which usually strikes people who are middle-aged or older, is different from the juvenile form and tends to have more severe effects, although its course is unpredictable. It may affect the heart, lungs, eyes, and other organs as well as the joints. It is treated with aspirin, NSAIDs, and other drugs. Physical therapy, heat, and adequate rest are important for people of all ages. Surgical replacement of severely damaged, useless joints allows many people with arthritis to regain the use of their limbs.

14

Cancer

Cancer takes in about 100 different diseases, but they all have at least one characteristic in common. Healthy cells that make up the body grow, divide, and replace themselves in an orderly way. Cancers are the result of cells that lack controls to stop the growth process, so they continue to multiply without restraint. Cancer cells compete with normal, healthy cells for body nutrients and space. They invade nearby structures, and they can also break away and spread to other parts of the body, even parts that are distant from the original cancers. A secondary growth is called a *metastasis* (plural: metastases). Cancer can develop at any age anywhere in the body. Success rates for treatment depend on factors such as the kind of cancer and how early it is detected. For example, the five-year survival rate for liver cancer is only 6 percent, while for bladder cancer that has not spread, the rate is 93 percent. Most skin cancers, which can be detected early, can be surgically removed before they do any damage.

Some risks for developing cancer such as increased age or inborn predisposition cannot be avoided. But many cancers are linked to factors that you can control. Smoking causes about 30 percent of all cancer deaths in the United States, and smoking is the cause of more than 80 percent of all lung cancers. Asbestos, arsenic, and other chemicals in the environment can cause cancer, as does radiation. Other controllable risks for some kinds of cancer include diets that are high in fat and low in fiber, excessive use of alcohol, and exposure to the sun.

Cancer is such a scary word for some people that they are afraid to seek treatment when they are suspicious of a problem. Although much remains to be learned about cancer, prevention and treatment greatly improve year after year. Many people recover from cancer in various organs and at stages in the disease where cure was once thought to be impossible.

Treatments for cancer include one or more of the following: surgery, chemotherapy, and radiation. Radiation therapy can be admin-

When Mel complained of pains in his upper leg, his family thought he might have arthritis. Even his doctor was not certain about the cause of the pain until an X ray was followed by a biopsy, in which a piece of tissue was removed and examined under a microscope. The biopsy showed that Mel had osteosarcoma, cancer of the bone.

Since the chances of a young person having cancer are slight, Mel found it hard to believe that this was happening to him. After talking to his doctor and a social worker, he began to feel better and to make plans for a life that would revolve around treatments. Mel met another boy his age who had to have his leg removed and who visited patients at the hospital to show them how he had recovered. This boy is now able to swim, ride his bike, and carry on a normal and productive life. No matter what the treatment—radiation, chemotherapy, and/or surgery—Mel decided he can deal with the problem.

istered to cancerous tumors by radioactive chemicals, such as cobalt and radium, or by powerful X-ray equipment. Rays alter the genetic substance within the wildly growing cancer cells, prevent them from multiplying, and destroy them. Chemotherapy is the use of drugs to destroy cancer cells. Different types of these drugs destroy different stages of the lives of cancer cells and hold them in check.

The most common signs of cancer are:

• Change in bowel or bladder habits
• A sore that does not heal
• Unusual bleeding or discharge
• Thickening or lump in breast or elsewhere
• Indigestion or difficulty in swallowing
• Obvious change in wart or mole
• Nagging cough or hoarseness

These signs and symptoms can be caused by cancer or by a number of other problems. Any one of these symptoms is not a sure sign of cancer, but if a symptom persists for more than two weeks, it is important to see a doctor. Pain is not an early sign of cancer.

In many cases, attempts to kill cancer cells cause harm to some normal tissue. Loss of hair is an example of a side effect from both radiation and chemotherapy, but it is temporary. Other unpleasant or potentially harmful side effects, such as nausea, vomiting, and infections, may occur, but discomfort can be alleviated and infections prevented or cured. Many support groups exist for helping people cope with the physical and emotional problems of having a serious illness. Therapy such as meditation, biofeedback (techniques that use instruments to detect and amplify signals from body processes) and hypnosis can lessen pain and hasten recovery in many cases.

Cancer treatment successes are improving steadily, largely due to advanced detection techniques, but the number of actual cancer cases is rising. In spite of billions of dollars and countless hours of research, the war against cancer has not been won.

BONE CANCER

Bone cancer and cancer of the connective tissue are relatively rare, but most of these cancers occur in young people under the age of twenty. The most common symptoms are pain and swelling in the bones and joints. Osteosarcoma is the type that originates in the cells that form bone tissue, and it is found most commonly in the legs. Chemotherapy has dramatically improved the ability to treat the spread of bone cancer, and the survival rate is over 70 percent.

Ewing's sarcoma, which develops in the bone marrow, usually affects the shafts of long bones. It is usually treated by radiation therapy followed by chemotherapy. In some cases, surgical removal of a limb is necessary.

In some cases, cancer from other parts of the body spreads to the bones.

BREAST CANCER

Breast cancer is the most common form of cancer in women. Warning signs include any persistent breast changes, such as a lump, thickening of tissue, pulling or dimpling of skin, nipple changes, or changes in breast shape or contour. Self-examination is important, since early detection is a major factor in curing breast cancer. The American Cancer Society or a local doctor can provide information on how to do a self-examination. Mammography is considered one of the most important screening and diagnostic tools. Self-examination once a month, a doctor's annual examination, and mammography should be used in combination. About 90 percent of localized breast cancer is now cured.

CERVICAL CANCER

Cervical cancer (cancer of the mouth of the uterus) has dramatically declined with the use of Pap smears, the microscopic examination of cells shed from the surface of the cervix. The risk of cervical cancer is greatly increased by becoming sexually active at an early age and by having multiple sex partners. Treatment is usually surgery and/or radiation, depending on the extent of the disease.

COLON CANCER

Cancer of the colon is one of the most common kinds of cancer in the United States. Its incidence rises sharply after the age of fifty, so older people are at risk; others at risk are those individuals who have a family history of one of the inherited colon cancer syndromes and those with ulcerative colitis. Studies have suggested that a diet high in fat and animal protein and low in fiber may contribute to the development of colon cancer. When cancer develops in the upper part of the colon where the contents are liquid, it may grow large without producing noticeable symptoms for a long time. Changes in bowel habits, alternating constipation and diarrhea, pain, and blood in the stools are warnings that should not be ignored. Doctors suggest routine screening for people who are at risk for developing colon cancer, even if they have no symptoms, since early detection means a greater likelihood of cure. A simple test is done to detect very small amounts of blood in the stool. By examining the colon with an instrument called a sigmoidoscope, doctors can detect about two-thirds of colon cancers. Growths in the colon can also be detected by means of X rays. Colon cancer is treated by surgery.

LEUKEMIA

Leukemia is a cancer of the blood-forming tissues, and it includes a number of different types. Large numbers of abnormal white blood cells accumulate in the bone marrow, squeezing out normal cells and suppressing their production. The leukemic cells are also carried in the blood throughout the body, and they can cause enlargement of the liver, lymph nodes, and other organs. Diminished numbers of normal cells result in the following symptoms: anemia, bleeding gums, tiny red spots on the skin, recurrent infections, fever, weakness, and pain.

There is no satisfactory treatment for some types of leukemia, but for the type known as *acute lymphoblastic leukemia* (also called acute lymphocytic leukemia), or ALL, the outlook is good. This is the most common childhood malignancy, with the highest incidence in children between the ages of three and five. Most children are helped by treatment, and more than half can be completely cured. Treatment consists of chemotherapy to kill the leukemic cells, and in some cases, bone marrow transplant. In bone marrow transplants, healthy bone marrow from a compatible donor is injected into the person with leukemia. Antibiotics may be needed to treat infection, and blood transfusions may be given to combat anemia.

LIVER CANCER

Liver cancer is rare, but about half of the individuals in North America who develop liver cancer have cirrhosis (see chapter 3). The risk of developing this types of cancer is high in people with chronic hepatitis B (see chapter 3).

The most common type of liver cancer is metastatic, originating in other organs and spreading through the bloodstream to the liver. The most frequent primary sites are the lung, colon, breast, pancreas, and stomach. Treatment of liver metastases is not very successful.

LUNG CANCER

Countless studies have shown that tobacco smoke causes cancer. Lung cancer is now the most common cause of death from cancer in both men and women. A person who has smoked two packs of cigarettes a day for twenty years is sixty to seventy times more likely to develop lung cancer than someone who has never smoked. Eighty to 90 percent of people with lung cancer are smokers. The risk is greater if the person began to smoke before age fifteen, has smoked more than a pack a day, and has been smoking for many years. Other risk factors are a family history of lung cancer and exposure to other cancer-causing substances such as asbestos or coal dust.

Treatment consists of surgery, radiation, chemotherapy, or a combination of these, depending on the extent of the disease. A cure is possible if the cancer is discovered early. But because it does not usually cause symptoms in its early stages, lung cancer is often not detected until it has advanced and spread to other organs. At this point, the outlook for long-term survival is poor.

Lung cancer can be prevented in most people. The best solution is not to start smoking, because it is very difficult to quit. But studies have shown that even if you have been smoking for years, you decrease your risk of cancer significantly if you stop smoking.

LYMPHOMA

Lymphoma is cancer arising in the lymph glands, nodes found throughout the body, which consist of lymphocytes and other cells that help defend against infection. *Hodgkin's disease* is a type of lymphoma that occurs mainly in young adults between the ages of fifteen and thirty-six, and also in people over fifty. The first sign is usually painless swelling of the cervical lymph nodes, or the glands in the neck. Glands in the armpit and groin may also be enlarged. Later, glands in the chest, abdomen, and elsewhere in the body are affected. Itching, fever, night sweats, and pain are other symptoms. A lymph node biopsy and other tests are done to confirm the diagnosis and to determine how far the disease has progressed. This kind of cancer has a high cure rate after treatment, which usually consists of radiation and/or chemotherapy.

Non-Hodgkin's Lymphomas are a group of malignant diseases originating in the lymph nodes and other lymphoid tissues. Like Hodgkin's disease, they are usually discovered in and around the neck, armpits, or groin as swollen lymph nodes or painless rubbery nodes, or as enlarged tonsils and adenoids. Children with lymphomas may have shortness of breath and periods of coughing. Growths in the chest and abdomen may cause symptoms due to pressure on various organs.

These lymphomas are more likely to spread throughout the body than Hodgkin's disease. Treatment includes radiation and/or chemotherapy, and depends on the type of lymphoma.

PROSTATE CANCER

Prostate cancer is the second most common kind of cancer in men. The prostate gland encircles the uppermost part of the male urethra, the tube that carries urine from the bladder. Enlargement, causing difficulty in urination is common in older men (see chapter 11), but it is not necessarily a sign of cancer. Prostate cancer progresses slowly, and may cause no symptoms. Enlargement is a late sign of cancer. For this reason, routine tests by doctors are recommended for older men.

SKIN CANCER

Skin cancer has been on the rise recently due in part to increased exposure to the sun's harmful rays. Most people are aware of the importance of covering their exposed skin with lotions that protect them from sunburn and skin damage. Fair-skinned people are more at risk for damage than those with dark skins. In addition to sunburn and premature wrinkling and aging, the sun can cause skin cancer. One especially serious form of skin cancer is *melanoma*, which may appear to be a mole. Be suspicious of melanoma if one half of the lesion does not match the other, the border is irregular, the color is mixed with shades of black, brown, and tan, and it grows wider than the tip of a pencil eraser. It is a very dangerous form of skin cancer that can spread through the lymph glands, blood, liver, lungs, and central nervous system. Its most common cause is excessive exposure to sunlight, especially before age eighteen.

TESTICULAR CANCER

Testicular cancer is one of the most common cancers found in younger men. Early signs include a lump or swelling in one of the testicles, and sometimes there is pain or discomfort. All young men should learn from their doctors how to examine their testicles and carry out a self-examination each month. Treatment depends on early detection and is highly successful.

15

Disorders of the Blood

Blood transports oxygen, nutrients, water, and other needed substances to the tissues, carries waste products excreted from cells, and helps protect the body from infection and blood loss. It is composed of red blood cells, white blood cells, and platelets (blood cells that form the first stage of clots), which are carried in the liquid known as serum. The blood can be affected by diseases that are acquired and inherited.

ANEMIA

The symptoms of anemia are the result of an insufficient oxygen supply to the tissues of the body; they include fatigue, weakness, pale skin, shortness of breath, palpitations, and in severe cases, heart failure or shock.

Anemia may be the result of decrease in production of red blood cells, destruction or loss of red cells, or from abnormalities that reduce the capacity of the blood to carry oxygen. Hemoglobin is the substance in red blood cells that

112

carries oxygen, and iron is necessary for its production. When there is insufficient iron, not enough hemoglobin is produced.

Iron deficiency anemia is the most common type of anemia, and it often affects babies, children, and adolescent girls. Conditions that may cause it include too little iron in the diet, disorders that prevent absorption of iron from the digestive tract, bleeding from gastrointestinal ulcers, heavy menstrual bleeding, pregnancy, and blood loss from injury.

Treatment of iron deficiency anemia consists of correcting the cause. For example, many people eat a diet that does not contain enough foods rich in iron, such as meat, fish, poultry, and whole grains; improving your eating habits can help to cure this kind of anemia. Some people need to take iron supplements to correct their anemia. Severe blood loss may need to be treated with blood transfusions. If you feel tired or weak, it is not a good idea to treat yourself with iron pills; a doctor should always be consulted so that blood tests can be performed.

In other cases, anemia is caused by a deficiency of vitamin B_{12} or of folic acid, both of which are necessary for red blood cell production. Deficiency of B_{12}, called *pernicious anemia*, is usually due to a defect in the person's ability to absorb this substance. Since B_{12} is found only in animal products, occasionally pernicious anemia occurs in very strict vegetarians. In addition to the other symptoms of anemia, the most serious symptom of pernicious anemia is nervous system damage, such as staggering gait, numbness of hands and feet, and poor coordination. If pernicious anemia is not corrected, the nervous system damage may be permanent, so early diagnosis is important. People who cannot absorb B_{12} properly must take lifelong monthly injections of this vitamin.

Folic acid deficiency is more common than B_{12} deficiency and is usually the result of poor diet. It is often found in people who drink excessive amounts of alcohol.

Sickle cell anemia is one of a number of inherited disorders that cause abnormal hemoglobin. Sickle cell anemia occurs almost exclusively in black people, and to a lesser extent in people of Mediterranean descent. About 13 percent of African-Americans in the United States carry the symptomless sickle cell trait. The presence of the trait can be detected by a blood test. When the gene for the sickle cell trait is carried by both parents, there is a 25 percent chance that their children will be born with the disease. Because of the abnormal hemoglobin, the red blood cells become distorted into quarter moon or sickle shapes, especially when they give up their oxygen. Since sickle cells do not flow smoothly through small blood vessels, they clog the vessels, preventing blood from reaching the tissues. The sickle cells are very fragile and are destroyed more quickly than regularly shaped cells. Due to the blocking of blood supply, sudden crises strike, causing excruciating pain in the bones of the arms and legs, or in the back, chest, or abdomen. These episodes may last an hour or even as long as a week. Children with the disease may not grow as fast as their peers and are more prone to infections.

There is no cure for sickle cell anemia, and treatment consists of relieving the symptoms of a crisis with painkillers, oxygen, and fluids by vein or blood transfusions. Avoiding triggers can help those who have the disease. Overexertion, lack of fluid intake, drinking alcohol, and other causes of dehydration should be avoided. People with sickle cell anemia should also avoid flying and high altitudes, as well as cigarette smoking, because all of these decrease the oxygen supply, which in turn increases sickling.

HEMOPHILIA

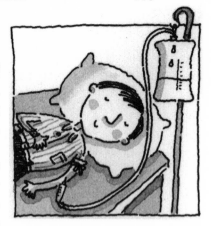

Hemophilia is one of a number of disorders that can cause abnormal bleeding. Hemophilia is a bleeding disorder that is inherited from mothers but occurs in males. Healthy men lack the faulty gene and are not carriers. On the average, a daughter of an affected man will have one abnormal gene and pass the disease to half of her sons, and half of her daughters will be carriers. In this disease, certain blood clotting factors are deficient or nonfunctioning, so even a minor injury can lead to severe bleeding. The amount of bleeding depends on the degree of clotting factor deficiency. The presence of the disease is sometimes initially discovered in newborns after circumcision.

Some hemophiliacs were infected with HIV, the virus that causes AIDS, along with injections of blood clotting factor before blood screening for HIV began in 1985. One of these people was Ryan White, a young man who gained recognition by working hard to develop awareness about AIDS before he died in 1990.

Today, the risk of hemophiliacs dying or being disabled is greatly reduced because effective treatment is available. Hemophiliacs can be taught to give themselves transfusions of factor VIII, the clotting factor in the most common form of the disease. They must be careful to avoid sports and other activities that might cause even minor injury. Severe bleeding into a joint can occur, resulting in severe deformity and disability.

LEUKEMIA (SEE CHAPTER 14)

LYMPHOMA (SEE CHAPTER 14)

16

Some Infectious Diseases

Infectious diseases are those caused by living organisms—parasites, bacteria, viruses, and fungi—that breach the body's defenses and invade it, producing a variety of reactions. The cells of the immune system attack and destroy foreign invaders, guarding the body against infection from both within and without. A healthy person lives in harmony with the many different microbes that normally reside in the body, but sometimes this balance is disturbed. When the immune system loses its battle, disease occurs.

AIDS

AIDS is one of the most publicized and most horrible diseases to have arisen in the twentieth century. It attacks the immune system, leaving the person defenseless against other diseases that would normally be conquered by the

116

body. AIDS stands for acquired immunodeficiency syndrome. About 1.5 million people in the United States are infected with the human immunodeficiency virus (HIV), or the AIDS virus. Many do not know it because they may have no symptoms for years. But they can infect others even though they look and feel healthy.

HIV is contagious, but it is not passed from one person to another by casual contact. It is spread by sexual contact and blood or other body fluids such as semen, vaginal secretions, and breast milk. Homosexual men and bisexual men (men who have sex with women as well as other men) who have had many sexual partners are at greatest risk for becoming infected with HIV. But the number of cases among heterosexuals has risen sharply in the United States since the disease now known as AIDS was first discovered in 1981. HIV-infected women can pass the disease to their babies during pregnancy or by breast-feeding. Drug addicts spread the disease by injecting drugs with needles contaminated with the AIDS virus. Prostitutes and drug addicts are responsible for many infections among heterosexuals.

The period of time before an infected person develops full-blown AIDS depends on many factors, but when the immune system becomes so weakened that it can no longer fight disease, infection can then gain a foothold in the body. In addition to numerous other infections, people with AIDS often get *Pneumocystis carinii pneumonia,* a disease called cytomegalovirus that causes blindness, and a cancer known as *Kaposi's sarcoma.*

Scientists are constantly working to develop vaccines and to find more effective drugs. Although advances have been made that allow AIDS patients to live longer, there is no cure for AIDS and no vaccine to prevent it. The only sure way to avoid infection with HIV is to avoid risky behavior such as unprotected sex and intravenous drug use that can lead to HIV infection.

EBOLA FEVER

The Ebola virus may be the world's most vicious virus. It kills over 90 percent of those infected; once the first signs appear, internal bleeding, shock, and death soon follow. The virus causes its victims to bleed from eyes, ears, nose, and every orifice; internal organs become almost liquefied. Although outbreaks of this disease have been limited to Zaire and western Sudan where the number of people affected is relatively small, its dramatic symptoms and mysterious occurrence make it especially frightening. The virus is spread from person to person through body secretions, so caregivers often become victims themselves. Scientists are concerned about the possibility of viruses such as the one that causes Ebola fever mutating into an airborne form.

FLU

Flu is the common name for influenza, an illness caused by a group of viruses. Usually people with flu have an abrupt onset of fever, muscle aches, headache, sore throat, cough, and chills and are sick for several days to a week. Antibiotics do not cure viral diseases so they do not help here. In a small percentage of cases, pneumonia and other complications develop. Vaccines made from killed viruses afford protection against the strains expected to be most common each year. Annual flu shots are recommended for people over sixty-five and those with chronic diseases.

INFECTIOUS MONONUCLEOSIS (MONO)

This viral infection is sometimes called "the kissing disease" because it is passed from one person to another through oral contact, as well as by coughing and sneezing. It affects mostly young adults and children. It is caused by the Epstein-Barr virus, and it is not highly contagious. Fevers, chills, sore throat, swollen glands, headache, weakness, and lack of energy are typical symptoms. Occasionally, the liver becomes enlarged. In rare cases, the spleen ruptures, causing sudden sharp pains in the upper left side of the abdomen; this is an emergency requiring surgery. Since the cause is a virus, antibiotics will not help. "Mono" usually runs its course in about two to three weeks with bed rest and plenty of liquids.

LYME DISEASE

A rash can appear three days to a month after a bite by the tick that carries Lyme disease, but only about half of the tick's victims develop a rash. Most develop fever, headache, sore throat, nausea, fatigue, swollen glands, stiff neck, and/or aching muscles. Weeks or months later, nervous system and heart abnormalities and arthritis may develop. When Lyme disease is caught at an early stage, antibiotics can prevent serious damage, but if the disease is not treated early, the person may suffer many debilitating symptoms.

Not all ticks carry Lyme disease, but those that do carry bacteria known as *Borrelia burgdorferi*. This kind of tick

Jody was reading a report at her desk when she saw a very tiny bug attached firmly to her arm. She was in a state of panic for a few minutes because she had read about Lyme disease and she felt sure that this was the kind of tick that carries it. She grasped the tick with a tweezers and pulled gently backward until it released its grip. She consulted her doctor, who told her to watch for an expanding rash and flulike symptoms for the next few weeks.

is commonly found on deer, mice, and other animals. Ticks are parasites that feed on the host animals, and they acquire the bacteria that cause the disease if these animals are infected. The ticks lie on grasses and low shrubs and transfer to animals who brush against them. They crawl upward on the animals, attach themselves to feed, and if infected, they transfer some of the bacteria to their hosts through their saliva or feces.

Lyme disease has increased twentyfold over the last decade. People who live in the northeastern part of the United States and other areas where it is common should take precautions. Prevention means wearing clothing that covers arms and legs when in wooded areas, fields, and gardens, and inspecting your body after possible exposure. Two Lyme vaccines are being tested at the present time.

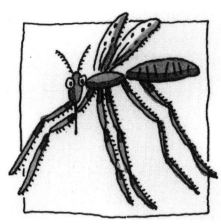

MALARIA

Malaria means "bad air" and was formerly thought to be caused by breathing swamp vapors. It is now known to be caused by a single-celled parasite that is spread through bites of infected *Anopheles* mosquitoes. It causes chills, fever, enlarged liver, and anemia. One form can attack the brain, lungs, and other internal organs and may cause death. It has been eradicated in the United States by programs that killed the mosquitoes that carried it, but it is still a problem in Africa, Asia, and Latin America. World-wide, 1 to 2 million children die from malaria each year, and about 400 million people suffer from the disease. Preventive medications are available for travelers to areas where malaria is prevalent. A new vaccine has been used in experimental tests. Several drugs are available for treatment.

PLAGUE

Many people use the term *plague* to describe an especially frightening and lethal disease that sweeps through large populations. Plague is actually a specific disease—*bubonic plague*—caused by bacteria called *Yersinia pestis*. This was the disease that caused the Black Death, an epidemic that killed half the population of Europe during the Middle Ages. The plague bacteria are carried by fleas that have bitten infected rodents such as rats and squirrels. The disease is transmitted to humans by the bite of an infected flea. The most common form is the bubonic form, which causes buboes (swollen lymph glands) that may ooze pus and blood, bleeding into the skin and other organs, high fever, delirium, and death, if left untreated. This form cannot be transmitted from one person to another. However, it may progress to another form, the *pneumonic plague*, which is spread from one person to another, and is highly contagious and lethal. Most people who contract bubonic plague in the United States are hunters or others who come in contact with wild animals. It is not a very common disease, but the death rate is very high if not diagnosed and treated with antibiotics within a day of developing symptoms.

PNEUMONIA

Pneumonia is a general term for serious inflammation or infection of the lungs. There are many different causes of pneumonia, but it is usually due to viral or bacterial infection.

Symptoms of pneumonia vary, depending on the cause and severity. They include cough, fever, chills, muscular pain, sore throat and headache, and varying degrees of difficulty in breathing. In diagnosing pneumonia, doctors listen for crackling noises in the chest and for characteristic dull thuds when they tap it. X rays sometimes show patches of air sacs filled with fluid and debris instead of air. Lab tests can be done to help determine the cause of the pneumonia.

Treatment depends on the kind of pneumonia. Overuse and inappropriate use of antibiotics are responsible for drug-resistant strains of pneumonia and other diseases. A onetime vaccination is recommended to protect against pneumococcal pneumonia.

RABIES

Rabies is a dreaded disease caused by a virus, and it is almost always fatal unless it is treated. It is generally transmitted to humans by the bite of an infected animal. The virus spreads from the site of the bite along nerves to the central nervous system, multiplies in the brain, then spreads to other tissues. Symptoms begin weeks or months later, with fever, headache, and malaise, then nervousness, agitation, muscle weakness, and other signs of nervous sys-

tem involvement. Rabies is sometimes called *hydrophobia* because
half of the people infected show a
fear of water (*hydro* means "water,"
phobia, "fear"). They have painful
throat spasms, difficulty swallowing, and frothing at the mouth; even
the mention of water triggers
spasms and salivation. Coma and
death follow within days.

Ken was bitten on the leg by a
fox that came into his backyard
from the surrounding woods.
He quickly called 911, and the
animal was captured, tested for
rabies, and found to be carry-
ing the disease. The doctor
washed the area of the wound
and gave him a tetanus shot
and antibiotics to control any
other infection. Ken was treated
with five injections over a period of four weeks.

There are no symptoms at the beginning stages of rabies, so pets and
wild animals that appear healthy
can carry the disease. Licensing and vaccination laws for
dogs and the careful control of strays have made dogs no
longer a major threat for spreading rabies. Many veterinari-
ans recommend the vaccination of cats, too. Most cases of
rabies are now caused by wild animals such as foxes,
skunks, and bats.

Anyone who is bitten by an animal should suspect rabies.
The animal, when possible, should be confined and examined by a veterinarian to see whether or not it is rabid. Rabies immunization is given as soon as possible after the
person is exposed.

SEXUALLY TRANSMITTED DISEASES (STDs)

Anyone can have a sexually transmitted disease without
even knowing it, although most have symptoms such as discharge and pain. Many people hesitate going to the doctor
or a clinic for treatment because they are embarrassed; but
what can happen if STDs are not treated early is far more
serious than any embarrassment.

STDs used to be called *venereal diseases*, or VD, and the

Megan's annual visit to her gynecologist alerted her to some unpleasant information. She had some warts on her cervix, the canal that leads to the uterus. It has been found that certain warts caused by the human papillomavirus can be a danger signal, because this virus may lead to cancer of the cervix. The doctor took a Pap smear and told her that a Pap smear test should be done every year in order to check for cancerous cells in her cervix.

two best known are *syphilis* and *gonorrhea*. Both are serious diseases that spread to other parts of the body if they are not detected and treated. Today, *AIDS* leads the list as the most well known and also the most deadly. (AIDS is discussed earlier in this chapter.) Some of the most common STDs are mentioned in the following chart. They are caused by a variety of organisms. Some STDs are spreading at a rate of 13 million infections per year in the United States. Two-thirds of the new cases are people under twenty-five years of age. The number of cases has been rising in spite of warnings about the danger of contracting them.

SOME OF THE MORE COMMON STDs*	
Disease	Approximate number in U.S. each year
Chlamydial infections	4 million
Trichomoniasis ("Trich")	3 million
Gonorrhea ("Clap")	1.1 million
Genital warts	750,000
Genital herpes	40 million affected, with as many as 500,000 new cases a year
Hepatitis B	100,000–200,000
Syphilis ("Syph")	120,000
HIV infection (AIDS virus)	45,000 new cases each year
*Based on information supplied by the American Health Association	

One of the most common STDs in the United States, *chlamydia*, produces no symptoms in about 80 percent of women infected with it. However, if left untreated, it can spread to the uterus, fallopian tubes, and ovaries, causing serious infection, pain, and scarring. This infection of the female reproductive organs, called PID (pelvic inflammatory disease) can result in infertility. A pregnant woman with a chlamydial infection can also pass the infection to her baby during delivery.

If you think you have been exposed to any sexually transmitted diseases, consult your doctor, family planning clinic, or local health department.

> If you are sexually active, look for the following warning signs of a sexually transmitted disease:
>
> - Unusual discharge from sex organs
> - Pelvic pain
> - Unexplained fever
> - Sores, bumps, or blisters near sex organs or mouth
> - Painful urination

WORMS

Pinworms are the most common worm infection in the United States, where whole nursery schools and kindergarten classes may be infected in a short period of time. Pinworms are tiny, white roundworms that infect about 4 million Americans each year, most of whom are children. People who are infested are plagued by a severe itching in the rectal area.

Since pinworms can be spread easily through contaminated drinking glasses, sheets, and other household items as well as from a person's

> Four-year-old Jason complained to his mother about an intense itch at his anus. He scratched so much she took him to the doctor and learned he had pinworms. Jason might have picked up pinworms from his sandbox, swallowing pinworm eggs when he later sucked on his unwashed fingers. Or he might have swallowed the eggs when eating contaminated food. The doctor explained that some eggs hatched in his intestines and two weeks later, a mature female laid eggs at night around his anus. This is what caused him to scratch.

hands, not just the affected individual but everyone else in the family should be treated with medication given by mouth to eradicate the worms. Bedding, clothing, and bathroom areas should then be cleaned thoroughly to remove invisible eggs.

There are many other kinds of worms that can infect people. The *giant roundworm* lives in the intestines and may grow to more than a foot in length. It is transmitted by eating soil containing eggs or raw unwashed vegetables grown in contaminated soil.

Most puppies are infected with *canine roundworms* and should be treated by a veterinarian beginning at the age of three weeks. Sometimes young children are infected with these worms after playing with an infected puppy.

The larval form of some roundworms, such as *hookworm* and *threadworm*, can invade the body through skin that contacts contaminated ground. This is a common problem in warm, moist climates where children often play barefoot.

Beef tapeworms, which live in the human intestine, can grow to a length of thirty feet. Although it is not common in the United States, the infection may be contracted by eating raw or undercooked beef. Cattle ingest the eggs, which hatch and are carried through the bloodstream to the muscles, where they form cysts (fluid-filled sacs). When the infected meat is eaten by a human, the cysts remain in the person's intestine and develop into mature worms.

Some kinds of worm infestations do not cause symptoms, while others may cause such symptoms as anemia or abdominal pain. Most can be treated easily with medication. Wearing shoes, avoiding contaminated food, and washing hands thoroughly before eating and after going to the bathroom are some ways to prevent infection with worms.

Childhood Diseases
and Vaccinations

Many of today's children are protected against the following diseases by vaccinations: measles (rubeola), mumps, German measles (rubella), polio, diphtheria, tetanus (lockjaw), pertussis (whooping cough), and *Haemophilus influenzae b* (a cause of pneumonia and meningitis). Doctors and community health clinics help parents with scheduling vaccinations, most of which should be given before a child is two years old.

CHICKEN POX

Chicken pox is caused by a virus and is most common among children ages two to eight, but it can occur at any

age. It is extremely contagious and is spread by direct contact and through the air. An itchy rash begins with small, reddish blemishes that develop into blisters and then form scabs. A chicken pox vaccine approved in the United States in 1995 prevents it in 70 to 90 percent of those who are inoculated.

GERMAN MEASLES (RUBELLA)

Rubella is a mildly contagious viral disease that causes a rash and swollen glands. Older children and adults may suffer joint pains as the rash begins to fade. Although rubella is a mild disease, a pregnant woman who contracts it may give birth to a baby with severe birth defects. The disease can be prevented by vaccination and is usually given to babies at about fifteen months of age. All women should make sure to be vaccinated before they reach childbearing age.

MEASLES (RUBEOLA)

Measles is one of the most serious childhood diseases; it is caused by a virus and is endemic throughout the world where children are not vaccinated. Beginning with coldlike

Molly's grandmother tells stories about having had mumps, measles, chicken pox, whooping cough, and other diseases that Molly and her friends never experienced and most likely never will. Early in the century, about two children out of ten could be expected to die before their first birthday from one of these diseases of childhood. Today, they are much less common in the United States due to vaccinations, antibiotics, and advances in medical care. Smallpox immunization was the only protective vaccination available for Molly's grandmother before she entered school in 1920. No one gets smallpox today; the World Health Organization (WHO) declared it eradicated worldwide in 1980, so smallpox vaccinations are no longer needed.

symptoms, measles produces a rash, fever, cough, and eye inflammation about ten to fourteen days after exposure. A child with measles feels very sick and may develop complications such as pneumonia or encephalitis. Measles vaccine has reduced the number of cases in children, but unvaccinated individuals of all ages still get measles.

MENINGITIS

Meningitis is an inflammation of the membranes surrounding the brain and spinal cord. It may be caused by viruses or bacteria. Bacterial meningitis, especially the kind caused by an organism known as meningococcus, can be lethal in less than a day. Patients may become desperately ill very rapidly, with sudden fever, headache, stiff neck, and rapid heart rate. An especially deadly form progresses to bleeding into the tissues, blood clots, shock, coma, and death within hours. Bacterial meningitis responds to treatment with antibiotics. Early diagnosis and immediate treatment are crucial when meningitis is suspected. Meningococcal meningitis occurs most often in the first year of life, and epidemics sometimes occur in closed populations of people, such as boarding schools or military barracks.

A vaccination is the introduction into the body of a small amount of killed or weakened form of a disease-causing organism; this material stimulates the person's immune system to produce antibodies to the disease without causing the disease itself. If the person is later exposed to that disease, his or her immune system recognizes and resists it. In most areas of the United States, children cannot enter school until they have completed their vaccination schedule. However, more immunization programs need to be enforced before measles, mumps, and other such diseases are completely eliminated.

MUMPS

Painful swelling of the salivary glands is the chief sign of mumps. It is a viral disease that can be spread by direct contact or through the air. Mumps is far more serious in adults than in children. It can cause inflammation of the testicles in about 25 percent of men who contract the disease after puberty, and in a few cases may cause sterility. Vaccinations are decreasing the number of cases.

POLIO (POLIOMYELITIS)

Polio, formerly dreaded before the development of a vaccine, is a very contagious disease caused by three types of virus that are spread from person to person by direct contact. Most infections cause only minor illness, but in a small number, the brain and spinal cord are affected, resulting in paralysis and occasionally death. The Salk vaccine has helped to almost eliminate polio in developed countries and is a very important part of inoculation programs. Polio is still present in some countries, however, and there are still occasional outbreaks in the United States.

TETANUS (LOCKJAW)

In countries where babies are delivered in unsterile conditions and mothers are not immunized, tetanus is one of the most common causes of infant death. About 560,000 babies die in Asia and Africa every year because their umbilical cords are cut with dirty instruments or the stumps are packed with dirt. The bacteria that cause tetanus are commonly found in soil samples from highly cultivated areas. In the United States, about 100 cases are reported each year, mostly in unimmunized people. Drug addicts who have used dirty needles or contaminated heroin are at risk.

The bacteria responsible for tetanus usually enter the body through a puncture wound contaminated by animal excretions, soil, or dust containing the bacteria. These bacteria then produce a toxin that attacks the nervous system and causes painful involuntary muscular contractions. Spasm of the jaw muscles accounts for the name lockjaw. Tetanus is fatal in more than half of the unimmunized people who contract it.

Babies are immunized with a combination for diphtheria, tetanus, and pertussis (DTP), and tetanus boosters for adults are recommended every ten years.

Suggested Reading

Aaseng, Nathan. *Autoimmune Diseases*. New York: Franklin Watts, 1995.

———. *Cerebral Palsy*. New York: Franklin Watts, 1991.

———. *The Common Cold and the Flu*. New York: Franklin Watts, 1992.

Aldape, Virginia T. *Nicole's Story: A Book About a Girl with Juvenile Rheumatoid Arthritis*. Minneapolis: Lerner, 1996

Anderson, Madelyn Klein. *Arthritis*. New York: Franklin Watts, 1989.

Arnold, Caroline. *Heart Disease*. New York: Franklin Watts, 1990.

Bergman, Thomas. *Children Living with Diabetes*. Milwaukee: Gareth Stevens, 1991.

———. *Children Living with Epilepsy*. Milwaukee: Gareth Stevens, 1991.

———. *Determined to Win: Children Living with Allergies and Asthma*. Milwaukee: Gareth Stevens, 1993.

———. *Going Places: Children Living with Cerebral Palsy*. Milwaukee: Gareth Stevens, 1991.

———. *One Day at a Time: Children Living with Leukemia*. Milwaukee: Gareth Stevens, 1989.

Biddle, Wayne. *A Field Guide to Germs*. New York: Henry Holt, 1995.

Byrnie, Faith Hickman. *Genetics and Human Health: A Journey Within*. Brookfield, Conn.: Millbrook, 1995.

Clayman, Charles, ed. *The Human Body: An Illustrated Guide to Its Structure, Functions, and Disorders*. New York: Dorling Kindersley, 1995.

Ferber, Elizabeth. *Diabetes*, Brookfield, Conn.: Millbrook, 1996.

Giblin, James Cross. *When Plague Strikes: The Black Death, Smallpox and AIDS*. New York: HarperCollins, 1995.

Harris, Ann, and Maurice Super. *Cystic Fibrosis: The Facts*. Oxford: Oxford University Press, 1991.

133

Hyde, Margaret. *Know About Drugs*. New York: Walker, 1996.

———. *Know About Smoking*. New York: Walker, 1995.

———. *Know About Tuberculosis*. New York: Walker, 1994.

Hyde, Margaret, and Elizabeth Forsyth, MD. *AIDS: What Does It Mean to You?* 5th ed. 1996.

———. *Know About AIDS*. New York: Walker, 1994.

———. *Know About Mental Illness*. New York: Walker, 1996.

———. *Living with Asthma*. New York, Walker, 1995.

Landau, Elaine. *Allergies*. New York: Twenty-First Century Books, 1994.

———. *Cancer*. New York: Twenty-First Century Books, 1994.

———. *Epilepsy*. New York: Twenty-First Century Books, 1994.

———. *Hooked: Talking About Addictions*. Brookfield, Conn.: Millbrook, 1995.

———. *Lyme Disease*. New York: Franklin Watts, 1990.

———. *Rabies*. New York: Lodestar Books, Dutton, 1993.

LeVert, Suzanne. *Teens Face to Face with Chronic Illness*. New York: Julian Messner, 1993.

Moe, Barbara. *Coping with Chronic Illness*. New York: Rosen, 1992.

Moragne, Wendy. *Attention Deficit Disorder*, Brookfield, Conn.: Millbrook, 1996.

Parker, Steve. *Medicine*. New York: Dorling Kindersley, 1995.

Parker, Steve, and David West. *Brain Surgery for Beginners and Other Major Operations for Minors*. Brookfield, Conn.: Millbrook, 1995.

Silverstein, Alvin, Virginia Silverstein, and Robert Silverstein. *Circulatory System*. New York: Twenty-First Century Books, 1995.

———. *Diabetes*. Hillside, N.J.: Enslow, 1995.

———. *Hepatitis*. Hillside, N.J.: Enslow, 1994.

———. *Mononucleosis*. Hillside, N.J.: Enslow, 1991.

———. *Rabies*. Hillside, N.J.: Enslow, 1991.

———. *Respiratory System*. New York: Twenty-First Century Books, 1994.

———. *So You Think You're Fat?* New York: HarperCollins, 1991.

Snall, Simon. *Living with Cancer*. New York: Franklin Watts, 1990.

VanCleave, Janice. *Janice VanCleave's the Human Body for Every Kid*. New York: Wiley, 1995.

Wilkinson, Beth. *Coping When a Grandparent Has Alzheimer's Disease.* New York: Rosen, 1995.

Yancey, Diane. *The Hunt for Hidden Killers.* Brookfield, Conn.: Millbrook, 1995.

Zonderman, Jon, and Laurel Shader. *Nutritional Diseases.* New York: Twenty-First Century Books, 1993.

For Further Information

Allergy and Asthma Network/Mothers of Asthmatics
3554 Chain Bridge Road, Suite 200
Fairfax, VA 22030-2709

Alzheimer's Association
919 North Michigan Avenue, Suite 1000
Chicago, IL 60611
(800) 272-3900

American Anorexia/Bulimia Association
293 Central Park West, Suite 1R
New York, NY 10024

American Cancer Society
1599 Clifton Road NE
Atlanta, GA 30329
(800) 227-2345
http://www.cancer.org

American Diabetes Association
P.O. Box 25757, 1660 Duke Street
Alexandria, VA 22314
(800) 342-2383
http://www.diabetes.org

American Heart Association
7272 Greenville Avenue
Dallas, TX 75231-4596
(800) 242-8721
http://www.amhrt.org

American Juvenile Arthritis Organization
1314 Spring Street NW
Atlanta, GA 30309

American Liver Foundation
1425 Pompton Avenue
Cedar Grove, NJ 07009

American Lung Association
1740 Broadway
New York, NY 10019-4374

Anxiety Disorders Association of America
6000 Executive Boulevard
Rockville, MD 20852

Arthritis Foundation
1330 West Peachtree Street
Atlanta, GA 30309
800-283-7800
http://www.arthritis.org

Asthma and Allergy Foundation of America (AAFA)
1125 Fifteenth Street NW, Suite 502
Washington, DC 20005

Autism Society of America
7910 Woodmont Avenue, Suite 650
Bethesda, MD 20814

Cancer Information Service
Building 31, Room 10A07
31 Center Drive, MSC 2580
Bethesda, MD 20892-2580
(800) 442-6237

Centers for Disease Control and Prevention
1600 Clifton Road, NE
Atlanta, GA 30333
404-639-3311
http://www.cdc.gov

CDC National AIDS Clearinghouse (NAC)
P.O. Box 6003
Rockville, MD 20849-6003

Crohn's and Colitis Foundation of America
386 Park Avenue South
New York, NY 10016-7374

March of Dimes Birth Defects Foundation
1275 Mamaroneck Avenue
White Plains, NY 10605

National Alliance for the Mentally Ill
200 North Glebe Road, No. 1015
Arlington, VA 22203-3728

National Association of the Deaf/Blind
814 Thayer Avenue
Silver Spring, MD 20910

National Digestive Diseases Information Clearinghouse
2 Information Way
Bethesda, MD 20892-3570

National Hemophilia Foundation
110 Greene Street, Suite 303
New York, NY 10012

National Institute of Neurological Disorders and Stroke
9000 Rockville Pike, Building 31
Bethesda, MD 20892

National Kidney Foundation
30 East Thirty-third Street, Suite 1100
New York, NY 10016

National Organization for Rare Disorders
P.O. Box 8923
New Fairfield, CT 06812-1783
(800) 999-6673

Obsessive-Compulsive Foundation
P.O. Box 70
Milford, CT 06460-0070

United Cerebral Palsy Associations
1522 K Street NW, Suite 1112
Washington, DC 20005

Index